WALKING THROUGH WALES

WALKING THROUGH
WALES

DAVID & KATHLEEN   MACINNES

DAVID & CHARLES
Newton Abbot   London

HUNTER PUBLISHING
New Jersey

British Library Cataloguing in Publication Data

MacInnes, David
  Walking through Wales.
  1. Walking—Wales—Guide-books.   2. Wales
  —Description and travel—1981- —
  Guide-books
  I. Title   II. MacInnes, Kathleen
  914.29′04858   DA735

  ISBN 0–7153–9044–9 (UK)
        1–55650–004–1 (USA)

© Text: David and Kathleen MacInnes 1984, 1987
© Line illustrations: David and Kathleen MacInnes 1984, 1987
First published, 1984
Revised paperback edition, 1987

Printed in Great Britain
by Redwood Burn Ltd   Trowbridge   Wiltshire
for David & Charles Publishers plc
Brunel House   Newton Abbot   Devon

Published in the United States of America
by Hunter Publishing Inc
300 Raritan Center Parkway   Edison   New Jersey 08818
Tel: 201 225 1900

We dedicate this book to the *Cymraeg*,
the Welsh people, whose kindness and courtesy
made our travels in Wales a joy

CONTENTS

ACKNOWLEDGEMENTS

We would like to acknowledge the generous, cheerful help of family, friends and acquaintances. Brian MacInnes from New Mexico did Snowdon, shepherded his father over the Cnicht ridge and did most of the Wye Valley Walk. Tom, Kathy (MacI) and Sara Flynn from Edinburgh (the latter, at 6 months, our youngest helper) walked with us on the North Borders and Snowdonia Walks. George and Doreen Foust from Pennsylvania helped on the Mawddwy and Berwyns Walks. Dana and Brownie Bergh from Vermont shared with us the Pembrokeshire Coast Path. Bruce Marshall of Dinas Mawddwy guided us between Corris and Dinas Mawddwy. Bernard and Betty Bramall from Old Colwyn Bay led us over much of the Carneddau Walk, and Alan Mattingly, Secretary of The Ramblers' Association, kindly introduced us to Welsh rambler groups and had some of our notes vetted. The Pontypool and District Ramblers, led by Bill Fielding and Glen Price, pioneered the way between Abergavenny and Pandy, and took us over that route on a happy, sunny day. The Mold Rambler Group provided route information for the Berwyns Walk over a delicious evening tea. Our thanks, too, to Howard O'Neill who kept us from the worst of our literary gaffes.

INTRODUCTION

Our aim in this book is to interest those who enjoy walking to return to the earlier, simpler days when walking was not just a recreational exercise but a common means of getting from A to B. At the turn of the century there was an upsurge of interest in taking journeys on foot. Gentlefolk took walking tours for the sheer pleasure of being in the countryside. They rested and refreshed themselves in a variety of inns along the way, and they paced themselves so as to have time to see the sights and sample the pleasures of each place through which they passed. This is a guide to just such walking tours through the 'wild Wales' of today.

We have chosen nine routes to suit a wide diversity of tastes and abilities. They range from an easy four-day stroll along the riverbanks and steep slopes of the Wye valley to a strenuous eight-day journey that climbs over the summits of Snowdon and Cader Idris. These journeys are mostly away from the road, taking you on ways in use long before the advent of the wheeled vehicles, going along rambler paths to high places and travelling on old tracks, Roman roads and the beds of abandoned railways. Overnight stops are at friendly B&Bs and country inns.

Wales has maintained its own identity as a country separated from the rest of Britain not only by barrier mountains but also by cultural differences evident to the newest visitor. One Welshman confided to us that it was 'cosy', by which he meant that it is geographically small and the people living in it are a culturally close-knit family. This comment reminded us of the Normans in Wales, and how, despite the mailed fists of their castles and walled towns, they failed to spread Norman writ beyond their walls because of the nature of the country and the character of the people. There is no doubt that something similar operates today, that Wales is still uniquely Welsh.

Wales is mountainous. It is hard to enter without climbing over a hill pass. You cannot move around without going up, down or

around mountains or, in the 'flat' south, without moving over rolling countryside. Human occupation was therefore forced into the valleys — for fertile land, for ease of communication and for protection from the weather. Hence Wales is a walker's paradise, filled with high, deserted country that provides solitude, beauty and challenge. At the same time, Wales never suffered the depopulation of the Scottish Highlands and, though it has great stretches of open country, no spot is more than half a dozen miles from habitation. It thus combines a strong sense of isolation with the sometimes comforting knowledge that one's fellows are not too far away.

A sense of history is strong in Wales. Stone Age man left stone circles, standing stones and burial cairns. Iron Age artefacts abound; hillforts occupy nearly every hilltop. The Romans left their roads, some of which you will tread, their camps and their forts. The early Celtic Church dominated Dark Age history and settlements grew up around their places of worship, reflected today in the many towns and villages beginning with 'llan'. The Norman conquest, still vivid in the minds of the Welsh, filled Wales with castles, and while the castles may now be in ruins, the memories of the swirl of rebellion and repression live on. Yet Wales today remains unconquered, as witnessed in the independent Welsh spirit, the living Welsh language, Welsh literature and the incomparable Welsh singing.

As walking tours are new to our generation, we have found people, even experienced ramblers, confused about the nature of our Walks. Perhaps it is easiest to start with what they are not. First, they are not a series of daily forays from a single base. Secondly, while they are long-distance walks, taking longer than a day to accomplish, they do not require camping out which eliminates the need for a heavy pack. Thirdly, they are not chosen with a certain number of miles or hours walking per day in mind, but as the route that best allows you to explore the attractions which each area offers. Fourthly, they not only obviate the need for a car, they require that your car be left behind, at home or at the starting point, to be used no further until the walk is finished. You will therefore not disrupt your relaxed pace.

11

For those who have not yet experienced it, such a way of travelling has unanticipated rewards. As your pace slows, your perception of the beauties of the countryside quickens—who can see a flower petal from a car or hear birdsong from a train? You will be aware of the inconveniences of other modes of travel—no looking for a layby from which to enjoy the view, no tantalisingly brief glimpses of the countryside from speeding conveyances, no disturbance from the mass media, no engrossment in the trivia of modern travel. As these civilised layers are peeled away, you are left with a leisurely love affair with nature—with the generosity of her views, the variability of her light and shadow, the caresses of her wind and rain, the profusion of her flowers and the variety of her living creatures. Your ties to civilisation will be limited only to the comforts of the secluded or busy places where you rest each night.

Using the Book

There are 9 Walks, each of 3 to 8 days' length, giving a total of 38 days' walking covering 374 miles (600km) in three areas: south, mid and north Wales. For ease of identification, the Walks are named after their local area (eg Black Mountains Walk, Wye Valley Walk). Each of the Walks is introduced with a map, and a listing of the sections (single-day walks), giving mileage and information on accommodation and public transport (for an explanation of the terms used in these, see Note A Accommodation and Public Transport, p155). The succeeding pages contain a general description of the Walk and of its overnight points. We can only give a brief idea of the riches each Walk offers; you may wish to explore further for yourself through the varied literature available (see Note F Further Reading, p166). The Walks are arranged in one direction of travel—generally north or, for circuit walks, anticlockwise—but they may, of course, be done in either direction. The introductory map (p6) shows the location of all the Walks.

Each day's walk (section) includes a brief overall description of the walk with a rating of the footing, detailed route-finding information and a sketch or two. The sketches are to help you visualise what you may see on the walk.

The heading of each day's walk gives the two overnight points, the distance and elevation gained (the difference between the lowest and highest points) and the Ordnance Survey maps needed. The distances and elevations will help you judge how strenuous the walk may be and how long it should take. The map numbers refer to the Ordnance Survey 1:50,000 series (1¼in/mile); for several Walks additional maps are also suggested and details given. While the heading gives the distance and elevation in both English and metric units, within the text distances are given in miles and height in metres. This is a compromise in order not to burden the reader with two sets of numbers everywhere. We chose the mile because it remains the most readily understood unit of distance and the metre because it is the unit used for elevation in the 1:50,000 series maps. The spelling of place names is taken from these maps and you may blame the Ordnance Survey if you feel that violence has been done to the Welsh spelling. An explanation of the terms used in the Walks is given in Note E on p165.

Other Walks

We have by no means exhausted the possible walking tours in Wales. We have selected, within the criteria of distance, accommodation and public transport, walks throughout Wales, away from the main roads, which give a wide variety of scenery and range of walking difficulty. Other tours may be made up. The Ordnance Survey maps conveniently give in red the paths having right-of-way. Local accommodation lists will help with accommodation, and nearly every settlement in Wales is served by bus. The Wales Tourist Board's *Walking in Wales* and W. A. Poucher's *Welsh Peaks* give many single-day walks.

BLACK MOUNTAINS WALK
South Wales
31 miles (50km) 4 days

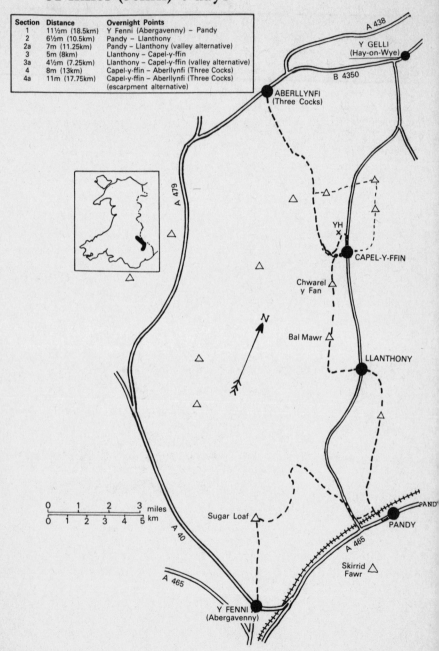

Section	Distance	Overnight Points
1	11½m (18.5km)	Y Fenni (Abergavenny) – Pandy
2	6½m (10.5km)	Pandy – Llanthony
2a	7m (11.25km)	Pandy – Llanthony (valley alternative)
3	5m (8km)	Llanthony – Capel-y-ffin
3a	4½m (7.25km)	Llanthony – Capel-y-ffin (valley alternative)
4	8m (13km)	Capel-y-ffin – Aberllynfi (Three Cocks)
4a	11m (17.75km)	Capel-y-ffin – Aberllynfi (Three Cocks) (escarpment alternative)

Travellers from Hereford will first see Wales as a great black ridge filling the horizon ahead. This is the most easterly mass of the Black Mountains. Some trick of the light turns its grass and heather flanks dark at any distance, especially in early or late sun or on cloudy days. Thus, aptly named, the Black Mountains have lured travellers for centuries. Their vast ridges have also been formidable barriers to Anglo-Welsh trade, as well as a past haven for turbulent Welsh princes who sallied forth into England for excitement and booty and returned into the depths of the hills.

The range is a compact block of some 80 square miles, bounded on the west and south by the Usk Valley, on the north by the Wye and on the east by the Golden Valley. Part of the Brecon Beacons National Park, it consists of four great ridges running northwest and southeast, all over 600m high, joined in the northwest in a manner similar to the Beacons, by a plateau that ends in precipitous north- and west-facing bluffs. The ridges are separated by verdant valleys, the most beautiful and best known being the Vale of Ewyas, the valley of the Afon Honddu. The mountains are broad, almost flat-topped, and are mostly covered with grass, heather and bracken; the highest points are only distinguishable when seen at a distance.

The human population is sparse, on small farm holdings, and there are no towns or villages. Holiday-makers are attracted in summer in considerable numbers because of the area's scenic beauty, the air of remoteness and the attraction of the romantic ruin of Llanthony Priory, deep in the Vale of Ewyas. It is also a rambler's paradise, with its miles of ridge walking and its secluded valleys. Most of the walkers will be found

15

on the eastern ridge, confusingly named the Black Mountain, because it is here that the long-distance Offa's Dyke Path runs in its 170-mile journey along the Anglo-Welsh border.

The Walk crosses the northeast portion of the range, beginning at Y Fenni (Abergavenny), a market town in the south, and ending on the river Wye in the north at quiet Aberllynfi, better known as Three Cocks on account of its ancient inn. You spend two nights in the Vale of Ewyas, one at Llanthony near or inside its ruined priory (depending on your choice of hotel) and the next at Capel-y-ffin, with its two chapels and ruins of a more modern monastery. The way is over Sugar Loaf Mountain to Pandy, then by the eastern ridge on Offa's Dyke Path to Llanthony, by the opposite ridge to Capel-y-ffin and finally up the Nant y Bwch Valley and down the steep northwest face of the range to farmland and forest leading to the Wye Valley. You will cover in all a fair sample of the delights of the Black Mountains.

Although the mountains are scarcely over 600m high, you may encounter cold wind, driving rain or mist on the ridge tops at any time of year. The ridges are broad and featureless, have only infrequent and generally inconspicuous cairns or other markers and the path is often indistinct. In poor visibility you may therefore have difficulty finding your way. So, in bad weather, you may wish to avoid the tops between Pandy, Llanthony and Capel-y-ffin by using the alternative valley routes we suggest. The way from Capel-y-ffin to Aberllynfi has only a short stretch on high country and can be safely negotiated in most weathers.

Besides the 1:50,000 series OS maps specified for each day's walk, you may use the OS 1:25,000 series Outdoor Leisure Map for Brecon Beacons National Park, 'Eastern area—Abergavenny and the Black Mountains'.

OVERNIGHT POINTS—Y Fenni (Abergavenny) is a busy, attractive market town on the river Usk. The ruins of an early Norman castle, dating from shortly after the Battle of Hastings, is on the south edge of town. It has a colourful history, being twice captured by the Welsh, in 1172 and 1215, the second time by Llewelyn the Great, and destroyed by parliamentary forces in 1645. The remains consist of two ruined towers, a gateway and a fragment of wall. More interesting than the ruins is the town museum, situated in the grounds of the castle. Other attractive buildings are the nineteenth-century Angel Hotel, the gothic-revival town hall, the King's Arms Inn, the King's Head Inn and the medieval church of St Mary. The cattle market, when the sale of cattle, sheep and other livestock is in full swing, is worth a visit. **Pandy** is a sleepy hamlet on the Afon Honddu near its confluence with the Monnow, unfortunately on the busy A465. **Llanthony** is set in farmland in the Vale of Ewyas (land of the sheep) bounded by the high grass and heather ramparts of the Black Mountains. It contains the ruins of an ancient Augustinian priory, a hotel built in these ruins and, nearby, another hotel, the two latter testimony to the attraction of the priory ruins and of the beauty of the vale. The priory sits nearly alone in the remote valley, with the stark walls of what was once a magnificent church and the remains of other buildings gathered round the green square of the former cloisters. The site is said to have had a cell built by St David in the sixth century, but the priory grew out of a small chapel built by a Norman knight, William de Lacey during the reign of William Rufus. As the story goes, William de Lacey wandered into the valley and was converted from his warlike ways into a man of peace. In a few years a monastic community grew up and the first priory chapel was built in 1108. The priory suffered from local civil unrest, especially during the reign of King Stephen, aided no doubt by the dislike of the local Welsh for the Normans. The present church and extensive additional buildings were erected at the zenith of the priory's life, between 1175 and 1230. After 1400 its fortunes declined and it ceased to be a priory after 1538. It has remained in private hands since, although the ruins are now under the care of the Department of the Environment. The priory church occupies the north half of the ruins. The west towers are still largely intact; indeed the Abbey Hotel occupies the southern of these towers plus what was probably the prior's quarters. Only the pillars of the church nave remain but the east end contains much of the transepts, presbytery, chapels and chapter house. South of the remains is St David's Church, built mainly in the thirteenth century, once the infirmary of the priory but, since the dissolution of the priory, an active parish church. West of the priory, across an open field, is the ancient gatehouse, a large stone building in fair repair, now part of the farm whose main buildings cluster round the priory. Staying at either of the hotels gives you leisure for a thorough visit to the priory ruins. It is accessible at all reasonable hours and is most dramatic when the early or late sun slants low across its old walls. These are also times when the ruins are deserted and you can dream alone of the bygone gentle life of ritual and prayer. **Capel-y-ffin** (chapel of the boundary) is in the upper reaches of the Vale of Ewyas just where the Nant y Bwch joins the Honddu and it is even more isolated than Llanthony. Yet it has three religious buildings: two small chapels and the remains of Llanthony Monastery (no relation to Llanthony Priory), besides a number of small scattered farms and the King George VI Youth Hostel a mile up the vale. The chapel close to the single-track B4423 just at the confluence of two streams is Anglican. It is a nearly square, white-washed building with a bell-tower much too large for it. Seven gigantic yew trees stand sentinel in front. To the east of the Anglican chapel and away from the road is a Baptist chapel, similar in appearance. Both have graveyards with some interesting epitaphs on the tombstones. The monastery is $\frac{1}{4}$ mile west up the valley of the Nant y Bwch. It was begun in 1870 by an Anglican clergyman, the Reverend Joseph Leycester Lyne, as a quite unorthodox foundation of the Anglican Benedictines. It lasted not much beyond his lifetime as a religious community and has passed through various hands and uses since then. It now lies in ruins except for a chapel built by the well-known sculptor, Eric Gill, in 1924. Both the ruins and chapel may be visited at any reasonable hour without charge. **Aberllynfi (Three Cocks)** is a hamlet in the Wye Valley on the A438 1 mile south of Glasbury. Beside the road is the historic Three Cocks Inn. It is a house of some antiquity and contains such old-fashioned devices as stair-gates and door-latches worked by bobbins. About 1 mile from Aberllynfi near Velindre, and only $\frac{1}{4}$ mile off your route, is an Elizabethan manor house converted into a hotel, the Old Gwernyfed Country Manor. Built around 1600, Charles I stayed there in 1645 when he was raising men and money in Wales during the Civil War. The house has many features, the most notable being the oak-panelled banqueting hall.

Old Gwernyfed

1 Y FENNI (ABERGAVENNY)–PANDY
$11\frac{1}{2}$ miles (18·5km) 1630ft (496m) OS 161

This is a perfect introduction to the Black Mountains, a walk of diverse scenery: over two mountains, one topped by an Iron Age fort, by wooded valleys, through hill farms and with a stop at an ancient pre-Reformation church so hidden from view that Cromwell's men could not find it to destroy. The way runs from urban Y Fenni (Abergavenny) to quiet Pandy and you will enjoy every step of it on a pleasant day. The views are tremendous from the hilltops, especially from Sugar Loaf Mountain.

We were led over this section by members of the Pontypool and District Ramblers, who had earlier found us the most interesting way between Y Fenni and Pandy. This was a pleasurable new experience as we had not walked with a rambler group before. We could not have chosen a kinder, more cheerful or more knowledgeable set of people, and the day remains a high spot in our 'research'. The steepest slope did not reduce either their good humour or their ability to chat. The way poses a modest challenge in route finding and the footing is good to excellent.

18

NORTHEAST—From the bus station in Y Fenni (Abergavenny) walk N through the main shopping area until you come to the war memorial. Cross the road and follow the shops, bearing R along the Brecon road. Continue past a garage and at the road junction take a road to the R. Follow this road (Chapel Road, marked further on) N past a crossroads. It becomes a lane and you climb fairly steeply to the Llyn-du car park, $1\frac{1}{2}$ miles from Y Fenni.

Stop for breath and a good view back to Y Fenni and the Usk Valley. From the car park take the L fork which leads you N through a farmyard on to a green track. The shapely cone of Sugar Loaf Mountain will be in view all the way to its top. After leaving the mountain gate, head towards the summit. As you near the summit cone, go R on a track that goes directly to the summit (596m), $3\frac{1}{2}$ miles from Y Fenni (Abergavenny). The panoramic view from the top is superb. To the S are three buttresses stretching like fingers (you came up between two of them) with Y Fenni (Abergavenny) beyond, and in the far distance is the Severn estuary. To the W is Pen Cerrig-Calch. To the N is the valley of the Grwyne Fawr and above it Partrishow Hill where your next destination, Partrishow Church, lies hidden. To the N, in the further distance, from R to L, stretch the great ridges of the main range, Hatterrall Hill, astride the Anglo-Welsh border, Chwarel y Fan and Mynydd Ddu.

Go E from the summit, descending steeply at first on rock and cross a heather plateau on a dry, sandy path. Follow the path down to a pony-trekking path at a stone wall and go L down to a road (5 miles). Go L past the tiny Fforest post office and shop. Go L at the first fork and R at the next to the intersection of five roads (Five Ways). Go L and cross the Afon Grwyne Fawr on Pont-yr-Esgob (Bishop's Bridge), said to have been built in 1188 for the visit of Archbishop Baldwin who was drumming up

Partrishow Church

19

Skirrid Fawr

support for the Third Crusade. Take the next fork R (signposted to Partrishow Church) and go immediately R through a gate on to a faint green track slanting uphill. Follow this until it becomes heavily sunken and go L to a line of trees, following them steeply uphill until you see a cottage. Head for a stone stile to the L of it and cross to a road. Go R for $\frac{1}{4}$ mile. Partrishow Church finally comes into view on a hillside opposite, above a steep ravine. As the road drops to the head of the ravine you pass the Holy Well of Mary on the R. Be sure to take the few steps down to it and dip your fingers in its clear, cold water. Leave the road and enter the churchyard by an arched gate (6$\frac{3}{4}$ miles).

The church dates mainly from the fifteenth century; the beautifully carved rood loft and screen are the principal features, but the faded remains of medieval wall paintings will intrigue you. Outside, near the stone bench along the S wall, is a preaching cross where the minister stood for outdoor services. The air of tranquillity and rural beauty will make you want to linger. We visited in late April and the daffodils were a riot of colour amongst the tombstones of the churchyard.

Continue E beyond the church to a track that leads you downhill through a farmyard (look up at the datestone below the twin chimneys of the farmhouse and see the date 1640) to a road. Go L and then R at the first side road, cross the Grwyne Fawr and pass the small Tabernacle church. Just beyond, as the road swings L, go straight ahead, crossing a wire fence carefully (you have a right-of-way and there may be a stile here when you pass). Climb steeply on grassland to a dirt track at the top of the rise. Go R, keeping a stone wall on your R. Ahead you will see Y Gaer, a hill crowned by an Iron Age fort. When the track forks, either go L on a track along the N side of Y Gaer or, if you want to visit the fort, head directly for the summit, rejoining the track on the E side of the hill. The track becomes a lane and drops steeply to the B4423 just by the Queen's Head Inn (9$\frac{1}{4}$+ miles). Go R towards Crucorney for about $\frac{1}{2}$ mile to a footpath sign. Cross the Afon Honddu on a footbridge and go R for $\frac{3}{4}$ mile on a path that goes under Great Llwygy Hill to a road. Go R downhill to a T-junction and cross to a path that goes over a railway line and a stream on a footbridge to the A465. Accommodation in Pandy is to the L.

20

SOUTHWEST—Walk S on the A465 from the Lancaster Arms in Pandy to a footpath sign R and take a path over the Afon Honddu and a railway line to a road at a T-junction. Take the road uphill for about ¾ mile to a junction and go L downhill. At the bottom of the valley go L at a T-junction across the Honddu to the B4423 at the Queen's Head Inn. Dog-leg R to a lane uphill to the W. It becomes a track that goes N of Y Gaer. After it joins a second track and beyond a stone wall, go L downhill to a road by a chapel. Cross a stream to a second road and go L (S) to the first lane on the R. This leads through a farmyard to a track uphill to Partrishow Church. Go through the churchyard to a road; then go L for ¼ mile, and beyond a cottage go L over a stone stile. Slant S downhill to a road, turn L (E) across the Grwyne Fawr to an intersection of five roads and turn R to Fforest post office. About 100yd beyond, a bridle path goes uphill to the R, signposted to Sugar Loaf Mountain. Shortly after it begins to follow a stone wall L, take a path R uphill past a copse of trees, through heather and over rocks to the summit of Sugar Loaf Mountain. From the summit go S to a path that goes SE into the valley between Rholben and Deri to the car park and lane that goes downhill to Y Fenni (Abergavenny). The distances are: the Queen's Head Inn 2 miles, Partrishow Church 4¾ miles, Sugar Loaf Mountain 8 miles.

2 PANDY–LLANTHONY
6½ miles (10·5km) 1425ft (435m) OS 161

This is a short day's walk on Offa's Dyke Path, from the busy Monnow Valley, with its railway and major road, into the depths of the Black Mountains. You leave Pandy by a path over the river and railway, climb on a little-used road and then by a faint path to the top of Hatterrall Hill, the first top on the long eastern ridge of the range which stretches northwest to near Hay-on-Wye. From the summit you continue over a gently undulating ridge astride the Anglo-Welsh border. The views east of the neatly hedged rolling English farmland of Herefordshire contrast with views west of the less-developed Welsh valleys and the untamed

21

ridges of the Black Mountains range. Hatterrall Hill broadens as you travel north, cutting off the near views, and it is not until you swing to the western edge of the ridge before descending to Llanthony that the isolated Vale of Ewyas opens up below, with Llanthony Priory as its centrepiece. You will be following Offa's Dyke Path from Pandy until you leave the ridge, but this section does not coincide with the turf wall and ditch of the ancient dyke. You will, however, pass one ancient monument, the grassy walls of a hillfort, as you climb Hatterrall Hill. The way is easy to follow, the footing good.

On the way up to the ridge, we came upon a hedger busy at his work. We had many times admired the finished hedges elsewhere in Wales: the carefully bent saplings or pleches woven around vertical or slanting stakes into a living fence. Welsh courtesy overcame the hedger's irritation at being interrupted and he slowed his work to explain the process. We learned that each district has its distinctive style, that many types of tree and shrub can be used and that you can tell how old a hedge is if you know what to look for. He felt that a well-made hedge was vastly superior to wire or stone for keeping sheep in. Hedging is hard work and requires considerable skill, and we were sorry to learn that mechanical hedge trimmers were reducing the number of traditional hedges.

NORTHWEST—100yd S of the Lancaster Arms on the A465 at Pandy a footpath sign marked 'Talybont' and a stile leads you $\frac{1}{4}$ mile across a meadow and over the river Honddu and a railway line to roads at a T-junction. There is an Offa's Dyke Path sign here. Go W uphill for $\frac{3}{4}$ mile to a crossroads (footpath sign) and R for $\frac{1}{4}$ mile to path L (another Offa's Dyke Path sign). The path leads to open bracken-covered hillside, the beginning of the long ridge stretching NW to Pen y Beacon (Hay Bluff).

Pass L of a small clump of pines and follow the ridge, keeping a farm track and farm to your L. You soon cross the ditches and grassy embankments of a small hillfort and climb past a large sheepfold, going either side of it, to a concrete survey post 2 miles from Pandy. Continue another 2 miles to the top of Hatterrall Hill (540m), an undistinguished summit on the ridge. You can not yet look down into the Vale of Ewyas,

but the Hereford countryside spreads out to the E. To the S is the
ascending ridge leading to your summit, in the distance the isolated peak
of Skirrid Fawr and, if the day is very clear, in the far distance the bridge
over the Severn near Chepstow. Descend from the summit past a small
abandoned quarry R to a modest col where there is an untidy pile of rocks
on a small knoll off to the R. The Llanthony path forks L (W) here, crosses
the broad ridge and slants NW down across the hillside along a stone wall.
The Vale of Ewyas comes into view as you come off the ridge and
Llanthony Priory is easily spotted 200m below. The path on the hillside is
a bit rough and wet in places. The wall peters out and is replaced by a wire
fence. You will come to a stile in the fence and a yellow arrow pointing L
into a field. Cross the stile, go down through a field and over another stile
into a wood, through the wood to a third stile and down a field to
Llanthony Priory. The Abbey Hotel is within the priory walls. The Half
Moon Hotel is 200yd N of the priory on the B4423.

SOUTHEAST—Go along the outside of the N wall enclosing the
priory ruins at Llanthony, reached by passing W of the priory and farm
buildings through an enclosed field. At the E corner take a stile into the
next field and follow its W and N edges to another stile with an arrow.
Cross and follow a farm track up through a wood to a third stile and an
open field. Keep along the fence on your R to the last stile and go R on a
well-defined path. This leads to the ridge top where you will pick up
Offa's Dyke Path. Go R (SE) over Hatterrall Hill, past a farm R and over
or past the grassy walls of a hillfort. Beyond, swing L past a group of pines
and by a stone wall down to a road. Go R for $\frac{1}{4}$ mile to the next road on
the L and go downhill to a T-junction. Continue straight ahead into a
field, cross a railway line and river and reach the A465 a short distance S of
Pandy.

ghosts

2a PANDY–LLANTHONY
(Valley Alternative)
7 miles (11·25km) 330ft (100m) OS 161

If mist covers the ridge tops before you start or if the day is simply too
windy, cold or wet, you may prefer a lower-level route. It is possible to
walk the Vale of Ewyas between Pandy and Llanthony and yet avoid
most of the busy B4423.
NORTHWEST—Retrace the **SOUTHWEST** route of Pandy–Y
Fenni (p21) between Pandy and the T-junction before the Afon
Honddu. Continue ahead past Cwmyoy Farm. Where the road turns L to
recross the Honddu, leave and take a track ahead, parallel to the stream, to
the farm lane to Daren. Go L on this lane and cross the Honddu again to
the B4423. Dog-leg L a few yards to a track parallel to the Honddu, past
Neuadd-lwyd and Sunnybrook, back to the B4423 just before it recrosses
the Honddu. Take the B4423 N ¼ mile to Llanthony.

3 LLANTHONY – CAPEL-Y-FFIN
5 miles (8km) 1480ft (450m) OS 161

This is an easy day on the main ridge west of the ridge on which Offa's
Dyke Path runs (Hatterrall Hill). We chose this as it is much more
interesting than the comparable stretch of the Hatterrall. It is narrower,
giving a greater sense of height and exposure, and provides better views
of the valleys and ridges on either side. You descend into the valley of
Nant y Bwch, going past the ruins of a monastery and the chapels at
Capel-y-ffin, all of which you may visit if you wish.

We met a group of walkers, mostly young boys, on the ridge, huddled
out of the wind for lunch. We asked one of the lads what he thought the
temperature was. He said 'cold'. We tried again, asking where they were
bound. 'To the telephone kiosk,' he replied. At least some are sure where
they are going! The way is easy to find, the footing good to excellent; all
you need for maximum enjoyment is a bright sunny day.

Capel-y-ffin

NORTHWEST—From the entrance of Llanthony Priory walk W through the small cluster of houses that is Llanthony village to an iron bridge over the Afon Honddu. Cross the bridge and bear R along the stream and through a gate into a muddy lane. Go through a gate on the other side of the lane to a tributary stream and follow its L bank until you can cross a footbridge. Keep to the R bank until the path enters a field and you reach a gate. Go through to a track and L through a farm. Turn L beyond the farm buildings through a field to a stile and a path running along the N side of Cwm Bwchel. Take the path and climb steadily but easily to the top of the ridge. At a large cairn you reach the ridge path (1 mile). Go R (NE) and climb, at first steeply and then gradually, to the summit of Bal Mawr (607m) and then to the summit cairn of Chwarel y Fan (679m) (3 miles). The ridge narrows as you climb, giving good views E into the Vale of Ewyas and over to Hatterrall Hill and W to the narrower valley of the Grwyne Fawr below the forested ridge of Mynydd Ddu. You will see ahead, faintly at first, the dam of the Grwyne reservoir at the top of the Grwyne Fawr Valley. Just W of the summit of Chwarel y Fan is a small evergreen forest, marking the summit from a distance.

From Chwarel y Fan continue along the ridge for about ½ mile to a large cairn. Go R downhill on a faint path that has occasional cairns. In ¼ mile you reach and follow the edge of a stony steep to another large cairn. Below you will see a large white building, the ruined church of Llanthony Monastery and the two clusters of yews beyond that hide the small chapels. Take a stony zigzag path down to the flat and go L to a small forest. Follow its W edge steeply down to a stile at its lower corner. If you are staying at The Grange, go L a few yards on a pony-trekking path. For the youth hostel go R over the stile and take a path passing above the monastery and go down along its E garden wall, cross a small stream and go through a tiny arched gateway to a lane, then R to the B4423 and L (N) 1 mile to the hostel. You will pass the Anglican chapel set in its mammoth yews just after you turn on to the B4423. A track leads R of the chapel 100yd to the second small chapel. If you wish to visit the monastery ruins (present owner welcomes visitors), go down The Grange access lane to the lane which leads you R to the monastery ruins. **SOUTHEAST**—Just S of the bridge on the B4423 at Capel-y-ffin take a lane W for $\frac{1}{4}$ mile. Go L through an arched gateway, cross a stream and go along the E wall of the monastery garden to a path W behind the monastery. Cross a stile and climb S along the edge of a forest. From its upper corner head across fields to a path that zigzags up the rocky face of Tarren yr Esgob. This path continues to the ridge path. Go L (SE) on the latter over Chwarel y Fan and Bal Mawr to a cairn on the saddle of Bal-bach. Turn L (NE) on a path, and when it forks go R and descend into Cwm Bwchel. Cross farmland and the Afon Honddu by a footbridge to Llanthony village on the B4423. The distances are: the ridge path 1½ miles, the Bal-bach saddle SE of Bal Mawr 4 miles.

3a LLANTHONY – CAPEL-Y-FFIN (Valley Alternative)
4½ miles (7·25km) 560ft (170m) OS 161

In the event of inclement weather, an alternative route along the Vale of Ewyas can be taken that avoids both the high ridge and the busy B4423. **NORTHWEST**—Take the B4423 NW from Llanthony Priory entrance and in $\frac{1}{4}$ mile take a R fork (the B4423 goes L) past Broadley Farm. Continue past several other farms, and at Vision Farm take a path that leads you by the two small chapels to the B4423 in Capel-y-ffin.

4 CAPEL-Y-FIN – ABERLLYNFI (THREE COCKS)
8 miles (13km) 1700ft (520m) OS 161

This stretch has great scenic variety: a narrow green valley in the heart of the Black Mountains, the vast grass and heather expanse of the northwest mountain plateau and a jumble of foothills with a maze of little wooded valleys below the plateau. The way over the mountain range is easy to follow but the route through the farmland poses an interesting challenge in route finding. Here you will need the OS map and our detailed route description in hand, as well as some native ingenuity in finding gates and setting courses. Losing the route here, however, holds no terrors, as you are never far from a road. The footing is good to excellent.

We encountered in the farmland here the only fierce animal in Britain since the wolves were all exterminated centuries ago. In crossing fields near our journey's end, we saw two huge bulls grazing placidly among a group of cows. Since the more intemperate of their race are supposed to be kept in solitary confinement we did not worry unduly but, discretion being the better part of valour, we kept close to a handy fence. The larger of the two raised his massive head, stared at us for a moment and then opened his great mouth to give (we thought) a bellow before charging. We stood stock-still, ready to clear the nearby fence in an instant. Instead, out of that vast throat came a tiny 'moo' and, as if ashamed of such a performance, the bull turned his back on us and retired to his grazing.

WEST—From the back (W side) of the youth hostel go S along a wall on a well-defined path to a fork. Take the L (lower) fork and descend gently, following a wire fence which is soon replaced by a stone wall made of thin stones thrust upright into the earth. The path leads around the S shoulder of Darren Lwyd on a contour and turns NW up the valley of the Nant y Bwch (brook of the buck). When the path meets the farm access road to Blaen-Bwch, go R through the farmyard to a track and then along the narrow path up the valley. (From The Grange go along its access road to the main road and go L to Blaen-Bwch Farm, joining the route from the youth hostel.) The valley narrows and the path steepens moderately at the top at 630m between Twmpa and Rhos Dirion, $3\frac{1}{4}$ miles from the hostel. You will momentarily expect the view of the Wye Valley ahead to begin unfolding. Instead, not until you begin to descend will the view open up and it will happen quite suddenly. Some 200m below is an open grassy plain sloping gradually NW. Further away, the land becomes a jumble of hills and valleys, the latter cut by tumbling streams hurrying down to join the river Wye. These hills and valleys are covered with a patchwork of farmland and forest. In the distance is the flat valley of the Wye itself and faintly beyond are more low hills. Leaving the col, the path steepens, and you soon turn R down the Rhiw Wen, which zigzags steeply down the face of the escarpment. When the gradient lessens, head W across the open grassland to the lane leading past Neuadd and Bryn-ddwy-nant, crossing a tiny valley and stream on the way. If you wish to avoid the interestirg but somewhat complicated stretch next, take the lane NW downhill to its junction with a road going L to Velindre. Otherwise, take this lane past Neuadd (farm sign here) to the next gate L. Go through a field and another gate and downhill to Velindre Brook (5 miles). Go R along the stream and pick up a green track leading to the farm buildings of Maes-y-lade Farm soon seen ahead. Go through the gate and pass below the buildings, picking up a well-used bridle path beyond, muddy in wet weather and rough in dry. Go downhill through a forest, crossing one forest track and going R at the second, which runs along Velindre Brook. This leads you past the village school (you will hear it at some distance if the children are in the playground) to the road (6½ miles). Go R to the first fork and L to a T-junction at the Three Horseshoes Inn in Velindre. If you are staying at Old Gwernyfed Country Manor, go L at the inn for ⅛ mile. Otherwise go R a short distance to a footpath sign and take a path L by some buildings and across a footbridge to grassland. Go N through several gates to a road and L on this road to a crossroads (signposts here). Aberllynfi (Three Cocks) is ¼ mile to the L.

Velindre

EAST—Just N of the Three Cocks Inn in Aberllynfi (Three Cocks) go R (NE) on a road for ¼ mile to a crossroads. Go R again ½ mile to a footpath sign and turn R across fields to a road at Velindre. Go R for a short distance to the Three Horseshoes Inn and L on another road. Just before the village school go L on a gravel forest track that crosses Velindre brook and goes along its N bank. In ½ mile take the first broad dirt track L slanting steeply uphill. This leads to Maes-y-lade Farm. Go out of the farm lane to another lane and go R uphill past Neuadd Farm and through a gate. Leave the lane when it turns sharp R and make your way across fields to a well-worn path, the Rhiw Wen, going up the face of the escarpment. It is a steep 200m climb. At the top you will be in a col with the path leading SE into a narrow valley. Look back at the view before you continue. Go down the valley to a farm, and through the farmyard to the farm lane. Shortly after the farmyard a path goes L hugging the S shoulder of Darren Lwyd, leading round to the youth hostel. If you are staying at The Grange or wish to visit the monastery and chapels in Capel-y-ffin, continue on the farm lane. You will pass The Grange and the monastery in about a mile. The chapels are near the junction of the lane and the B4423. To reach the youth hostel from Capel-y-ffin, walk N on the B4423 for 1 mile.

4a CAPEL-Y-FFIN –
ABERLLYNFI (THREE COCKS)
(Escarpment Alternative)
11 miles (17·75km) 2000ft (610m) OS 161

A slightly longer and more adventurous walk may be taken from the
youth hostel in Capel-y-ffin to Aberllynfi (Three Cocks) by climbing
back up to Offa's Dyke Path on the eastern ridge of the Black Mountains
(called the Black Mountain, confusingly), going NW to Pen y Beacon
(Hay Bluff) and then following the edge of the great NW escarpment of
the Black Mountains down to Bwlch-yr-Efengel (Gospel Pass) and up
over Twmpa (Lord Hereford's Knob) to rejoin the main route in the col
SW of Twmpa. It adds another 3 miles to your route and more height
(although once on the escarpment, the changes in gradient are small) but,
if you like ridge walking and distant views, it is worth the additional
mileage. It should not be attempted, however, in mist or bad weather.
NORTHWEST — Ask at your lodging for the best route to Offa's Dyke
Path going NW. Once on the Path you will find the ridge quite broad
and rather dull until you reach Pen y Beacon (Hay Bluff). There are good
views down to the Wye Valley but Hay is hidden by the foothills. A
hang-glider school often practises under Hay Bluff. The experts carry
their gliders to the top and you may see them circling high above the
bluff. Go L (SW) at the pylon on the bluff and skirt the bluff edge,
descending to Bwlch-yr-Efengel (Gospel Pass) and crossing the B4423.
Climb along the cliff edge of Twmpa to the saddle SW of it. Here you
will join our regular route from Capel-y-ffin and go R (NW) down the
escarpment. There will be no path between Pen y Beacon (Hay Bluff) and
the saddle but the way will be evident.

BRECON BEACONS WALK
South Wales
29½ miles (47·5km) 3 days (circuit)

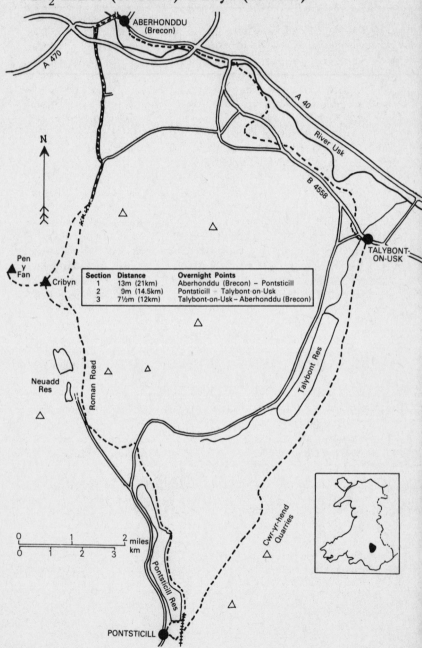

Section	Distance	Overnight Points
1	13m (21km)	Aberhonddu (Brecon) – Pontsticill
2	9m (14.5km)	Pontsticill – Talybont-on-Usk
3	7½m (12km)	Talybont-on-Usk – Aberhonddu (Brecon)

ACCOMMODATION
Aberhonddu (Brecon) bus (National Welsh) Abergavenny 9 r/t dly Mon–Sat, 2 r/t Sunday, bus

Pontsticill (by Merthyr Tydfil)	Penrhadwy House West (PH) tel (0685) 4187
	Ystradgynwyn, Torpentau (PH) tel (0685) 2158
	Pengell (F) tel (0685) 2169
Talybont-on-Usk	Usk Hotel tel (087487) 251
	Aberclydach (GH) tel (087487) 237
	Brynhyfryd (GH) tel (087487) 230
	Coity Mawr (GH) tel (087487) 664
	Brynoyre Farm ($\frac{1}{2}$m on Talybont Res Rd) tel (087487) 250

PUBLIC TRANSPORT
Aberhonddu (Brecon) bus (national Welsh) Abergavenny 9 r/t dly Mon–Sat, 2 r/t Sunday, bus (National Welsh) Hereford 6 r/t dly Mon–Sat
Pontsticill train (Brecon Mountain Railway) Pant, for bus to Merthyr Tydfil, freq service mid May–mid Sept
Talybont-on-Usk bus (National Welsh) Abergavenny, Brecon 9 r/t dly Mon–Sat, 2 r/t Sun

---

This Walk introduces you to the famous Brecon (or Brecknock) Beacons, the mountain massif after which the surrounding National Park was named. The Beacons, formed of Old Red Sandstone, are characterised by long north–south ridges which rise gently from the south to their highest points and then plunge boldly in steep north-facing cliffs, somewhat like sharp-prowed ships sinking by their sterns. They have the amazing quality of appearing different each time they are viewed. Changes in the weather or the level of the sun seem to alter their contours and one never tires of looking at them. The most dramatic view is from Brecon, from where the great north faces are best seen. The Beacons themselves, except for these northern cliffs, are mostly vast grassy moorlands, surrounded by rolling farmland on all sides. Their Welsh name, Bannau Brycheiniog, is from an Irish king, Brychan, who came here in that obscure period after the Romans had departed and left a vast progeny, reputed to be 12 sons and 24 daughters, almost all of whom led a religious life. His descendants, aided by the geographical isolation of the area, protected by the Beacons and other mountains, helped keep the area an independent kingdom until well into the tenth century.

The Walk is a circuit which can be started at any of the three overnight points, although the southern point, Pontsticill, is more difficult to reach by public transport. The route goes through the full length of the Beacons, climbs two of the three highest peaks, crosses the hills at the lower end of the Park and then idles along a section of the Monmouthshire and Brecon Canal. You will cover great areas of open moorland, some of it on an old Roman road; stand on high peaks with marvellous views; walk on the bed of an old tramway, precursor of the railways; pass through a deep forest and stroll along a canal towpath in the

Usk Valley, sampling much of what south Wales has to offer in scenic variety and walking challenges.

The Walk is easy to reach by public transport and, being a circuit, you need only one point for start and finish.

It is possible to combine this Walk with time spent at a course of study at the Brecon Beacons National Park Study Centre at Danywenallt, 1½ miles from Talybont, a few yards off our route. Courses include natural history, exploring and landscape painting. Enquiries about the Study Centre should be addressed to the National Park Officer, Glamorgan St, Brecon, Powys LD3 7DP (tel (0874) 2311 and 3378).

Besides the OS maps specified in each section (1:50,000 series) there is an OS 1:25,000 series Outdoor Leisure Map for this Walk, 'Brecon Beacons National Park, Central Area, Brecon and the Beacons'.

OVERNIGHT POINTS — Aberhonddu (Brecon) is one of the fine old towns of Wales. The Romans built a fort nearby and the Normans under Bernard Newmarch, half-brother of William the Conqueror, built a castle here 25 years after the Conquest. The Priory of St John the Evangelist was started about the same time and parts of the first church are included in the present cathedral which was built during the thirteenth and fourteenth centuries. The first borough charter was granted in 1246. Christ College, a well-known public school, was founded by Henry VIII in 1541. The Brecon fairs, started in 1366 for trade, hiring and pleasure, continue in two funfairs each year in May and November. There is much to see and do and you can easily spend an extra day here. The Promenade is a riverside walk along the Usk, with fine views of the Beacons, a bowling green, tennis courts, refreshments, boats for hire or short cruises. There is a short walk from the cathedral through the Groves, a wooded dingle with a nature trail. From the cathedral you can also climb up Crug Hill to visit a large well-preserved earthwork which was built by the Celts about 100 BC. You can view the remains of Brecon Castle from the gardens of the Castle of Brecon Hotel, visit the cathedral, the Museum of the 24th Regiment (South Wales Borderers) or the Brecknock Museum which illustrates the early life of the area. On market days the cattle market is worth a visit just to watch the auction in action. In the evening there may be a performance at the Brecknock Little Theatre. **Talybont-on-Usk** is a quiet village in the valley of the river Usk on the Monmouthshire–Brecon Canal at the point where the canal crosses the Afon Caerfanell. It is set in farmland surrounded by high hills bristling with pines and has an aura of peace not seriously disturbed by the occasional holiday boaters on the canal, the fishermen heading for the Talybont Reservoir or the holiday-makers enjoying the local restaurants and scenery. **Pontsticill** is a hamlet below the Pontsticill Reservoir at the southern boundary of the Park. It is only a few miles from the heavily populated Merthyr Tydfil Valley. Indeed, at night the valley lights are bright in the distance, but the village is on the edge of the Park moorland in a sparsely settled area and the madding crowd seems far away. Nearby, at the reservoir dam, is the northern terminus of the Brecon Mountain Railway, one of the 'Little Railways' of Wales.

1 ABERHONDDU (BRECON)– PONTSTICILL
13 miles (21km) 1510ft (460m)
14½ miles (23·5km) 2450ft (745m) via Pen y Fan OS 161

The longest day of the Walk goes by a Roman road, which once led from the Roman fortress of Y Gaer just west of Brecon south to Cardiff, and by the bed of an abandoned railway. It is possible to include two Brecon Beacon peaks by digressing a bit off the main route. The old railway on which you will tread was the Brecon–Merthyr line which operated from 1863 to 1956. It ended the isolation of the farms around Brecon and the Usk Valley and changed the pattern of farming by opening up to them the Merthyr markets. Before the railway the farms had only the local markets for their produce and the people rarely travelled beyond the bounds of their local area. The way is easy to follow, the footing excellent.

Brecon's past and future

SOUTH—Walk W along Ship Street from the centre of Aberhonddu (Brecon). It becomes Bridge Street and you cross the river. In ½ mile go L at a sign to St David's Hospital and take a road past the hospital and over the A40 bypass. The road narrows and climbs through farmland. At 2½ miles you pass a road L to Cantref and at 3 miles you reach a T-junction. Go R for ¾ mile. The tarmac ends and a rough, rocky track continues between trees. You soon emerge through a gate into open land. The Roman road, a well-worn rocky track, goes S uphill along the E slope of Bryn-teg (fair hill), a buttress of Cribyn. A path diverges R and climbs the buttress. If you take the Roman road you climb easily to the steep head of the great Cwm Cynwyn and pass through a notch (600m, 6 miles from Brecon). If you take the path up Bryn-teg to Cribyn you will climb somewhat more steeply for $1\frac{1}{2}$ miles to its summit (795m). It is the Beacons' third highest peak. From Cribyn you can turn S and then SE on a path along the edge of Craig Cwm Cynwyn back to the Roman road at the notch. This digression to Cribyn adds about $\frac{1}{3}$ mile and an additional 195m climb to your journey. The even sturdier walker can turn W from Cribyn and climb along the Craig Cwm-Sere to Pen y Fan (886m), the highest peak of the Beacons and of south Wales, returning via Cribyn to the notch. This adds another $1\frac{1}{2}$ miles and 90m climb to the route. Either peak will give you magnificent views. To the N you may see the Cader Idris range and Plynlimon. To the W is Carmarthen Fan and E are the Black Mountains, making up the other two mountain ranges in the National Park. N of the Black Mountains are the hills of the Radnor Forest and between them are the Herefordshire plain and the Shropshire hills. To the S stretch the descending grassy ridges of the Beacons, beyond which are the crowded valleys of the south Wales coalfields.

From the notch, the Roman road goes S easily downhill along the flank of Tor Glas and past the two Neuadd reservoirs. At a deep ravine made by the Nant y Gloesydd you have a choice of crossing to the continuation of the Roman road or of going R downhill a short distance to the abandoned railway, built to assist the construction of the reservoirs, where you go L on the old railway bed. Both alternatives reach the dam access road in about $\frac{1}{2}$ mile. Go along the road a short distance and take the railway bed where it diverges L. You swing E and enter the Taf Fechan evergreen forest. In 1 mile from the dam road you reach the junction of the reservoir railway with the Brecon–Merthyr railway line (now also abandoned) at the former Torpentau Station, the high point on that line. Beyond is a narrow road that runs between Pontsticill and Talybont. Cross it, pick up the railway bed on the other side and follow it S down to and along the edge of the Pontsticill Reservoir to the last station on the Brecon Mountain Railway by the dam (this railway is still in operation). Go R on a road across the dam and go uphill a short way to the Pontsticill–Talybont road. All the B&Bs are L except Ystradgynwyn which stands alone at the head of the reservoir. To reach it, leave the railway at the site of old Torpentau Station and go R downhill on the road for $\frac{1}{2}$ mile.

Roman road

NORTH—Go N from the Red Cow Inn in Pontsticill to the second road R and cross the dam of the Pontsticill Reservoir to an abandoned railway bed N of the terminus of the Brecon Mountain Railway. Go L (N) along the bed, cross a road to a railway junction and take the abandoned Neuadd Reservoirs' railway E 1 mile through a forest to where it joins the reservoir access road. Go N on the road until the railway digresses R, then follow the railway. Shortly after it crosses the Nant y Groesydd (trees and buildings L) take a path R 200yd to a track and follow this old Roman road L over a notch and down Cwm Cynwyn to a lane. Go N for $\frac{3}{4}$ mile to a T-junction and go L to Aberhonddu (Brecon) 3 miles away. When you reach the main road go R $\frac{1}{2}$ mile to the town centre. The distances are: railway junction 4 miles, notch 7 miles, lane to Aberhonddu (Brecon) 9 miles.

the Beacons

2 PONTSTICILL–TALYBONT-ON-USK
9 miles (14·5km) 1200ft (365m) OS 160, 161

This is a little-used moorland and forest walk over the high country between the valleys of Taf Fechan and Glyn Collwn. You will see the hand of man in a large limestone quarry, an abandoned tramway that served it, the blue waters of reservoirs, reforested slopes and a canal, but the general feeling is still one of undisturbed nature. You will enjoy good views from the moorland of the long rising grassy spines of the Beacons and of the Pontsticill and Talybont Reservoirs. One of the 'Little Railways' of Wales, the Brecon Mountain Railway has its upper terminus near Pontsticill and your way passes under it. Perhaps you may see a train full of holiday-makers puffing by overhead.

Part of the way will be along the abandoned bed of the old 12-mile-long Brynoer Tramroad, built in 1815 to connect the Rhymney Ironworks at Brynoer Patch with the Brecknock (Brecon)–Abergavenny Canal at Talybont. Also serving the great Trefil limestone quarries en route, the road carried coal, lime and pit wood until it was abandoned in 1865. Tramroads were horse-drawn railways, the precursors of the present network of locomotive railway. They solved, in an elementary

oldest living inhabitant

way, all the problems of later railways—track and wagon design, embankments, bridges, tunnels and traffic control, etc. Although in use before 1700, their rise was dependent on and coexistent with the spread of the canals for which they were feeders from collieries, quarries and ironworks. While early tramroads used wooden sleepers, wood or iron-topped wood rails and flanged wheels which were somewhat similar to modern railway design, by the time of the Brynoer Tramroad, cast-iron L-shaped rails or tramplates, held by iron chairs or saddles mounted on stone sleepers, were commonly used. The wagons had broad unflanged wheels which ran on the flat of the tramplate, held from sideways movement by the tramplate flange. Wagons typically held $1\frac{1}{2}$–3 tons, and one horse would draw 1–3 wagons, depending on the load and gradient of the track. The horses were hitched in single-file and walked between the rails on cobbles or gravel. You will find many of the stone sleepers still in place on this tram bed. All will have indentations for the iron saddle that held the rail. Only a few will have holes into which plugs of wood and nails were driven to hold down the saddle and hence the rail. You will find the gauge (distance between the rails) to be 3ft 6in. You will also notice several places where the bed is widened to accommodate double tracks for passing. As you travel you can well imagine the heavy tread of horses and the loud rumble of loaded wagons as the train was carefully braked downhill. You will pass the Cwar-yr-hend quarry, whose workings run for more than a mile, but the even larger Trefil quarries are several miles south of your route.

The way is fairly straightforward although the stretch between Pontsticill and the Cwar-yr-hend quarry is mostly sheep tracks and needs some care in route finding. The footing is good to excellent.

NORTHEAST—From the Red Cow Inn in Pontsticill, leave the main road and go R steeply downhill on the first road. Go over a bridge and past the Water Board buildings to a track L uphill between stone walls. Cross a road and continue uphill through a gate, cross an abandoned arm of the Brecon Mountain Railway and go under the railway. From the underpass the track, now green and faint, goes L a short distance and then turns R and follows a line of hawthorn trees uphill to a gate. Here red dots on stones lead you uphill into the open. When you cross a well-defined path, $1\frac{1}{4}$ miles from Pontsticill, ignore the red dots which continue ahead and go L on this path. It follows the contour but soon becomes intermittent. You will observe a stream flowing SW and then W into a small forest bordering the reservoir. Your way will be NE parallel to but above this stream. Keeping the stream on your L, continue NE until you reach quarry workings. Keep the quarry on your R for $\frac{1}{2}$ mile or walk along the quarry road until you see the quarry buildings ahead. Now look N and you will be able to pick out the distinctive small bluff of Darren-Fawr on the skyline about 1 mile away. Head for this bluff. On your way you will dip into a shallow valley with a circular marsh in its bottom. Go round either edge and you will soon pick up a well-worn track ($4\frac{1}{4}$ miles) that leads you up to and around the bluff. This track becomes a rough farm track and you come out to and cross the SE slope of the Talybont Valley. Here there are outstanding views of the Talybont Reservoir, Talybont Forest and the Beacons. Continue downhill in the open to the edge of the forest ($5\frac{1}{2}$ miles). Here a track comes up L along one edge of the forest, the bed of an abandoned tramway comes in from the R and goes along the forest edge ahead, while the farm road you have been on crosses the tramway bed and diverges R. Take the tramway bed NE along the forest edge. You soon enter the forest and go downhill on an easy slope until you reach the canal at Talybont. There are occasional openings in the forest, allowing glimpses of the Talybont Reservoir, the little village of Aber and the farmland along the Afon Caerfanell. Cross the canal by an old stone bridge at the tramway end and in a few yards reach the B4558 at the White Hart Inn at Talybont. For the Usk Hotel go R to the first road on the L. The hotel is $\frac{1}{2}$ mile along this road. Check for the location of your B&B.

Brecon Mountain train

SOUTHWEST — By the White Hart Inn in Talybont go up the canal embankment and over the canal on a stone bridge. Go SW on the old tramway bed (the middle of three ways, R to the inn camping ground, L to an abandoned railway). You immediately turn L over the railway and start a long easy ascent along the hillside on the tramway bed. Shortly after you come out of the wood, the tramway bed is blocked by the fill of a farm track. Take this track SW uphill and it will carry you past the E bluff of Darren-Fawr to the open moorland. The road soon forks and you go L. Ahead you will see the workings of the old Cwar-yr-hend quarry, stretching for a mile. Head towards the quarry buildings. The road becomes a track, skirts the W end of a marsh and reaches the quarry road. Go R on this road for a short distance and then go SW below the quarry debris. Here you will pick up a faint path on close-cropped grass, running parallel to the debris about 100yd below it. You soon see the stream in Cwm Criban on your R. Keep parallel to it (you may misplace the path, which is faint in places) until the stream swings W. Continue SW and climb slightly. When the copper-green spire of the building on the Pontsticill Reservoir dam is on your right, go R downhill to a gate in a wall and follow a line of hawthorn trees to a path L through an underpass of the Brecon Mountain Railway. Continue downhill over an abandoned railway and cross a road to a second road. Go R uphill to Pontsticill. The distances are: fork beyond Darren-Fawr $4\frac{3}{4}$ miles, quarry $5\frac{3}{4}$ miles.

3 TALYBONT-ON-USK—
ABERHONDDU (BRECON)
7½ miles (12km) negligible elevation OS 160, 161

This is an easy day on the towpath of the Monmouthshire and Brecon Canal where you will enjoy canal life even if you have no boat. You will see the major features of a canal—lock, aqueducts, bridges—and perhaps a canal pleasure boat or two as well as abundant birdlife. The canal wanders along the flats of the Usk Valley, never far from the river. It goes through woods and lush farmland right into the built-up part of Brecon. You may be lulled back a century to the early canal life and may half expect to see a narrow boat being pulled by a horse. The canal, opened in 1815 with its arterial tramways, was unique in being originally sponsored by the consumers rather than the industrialists. Even though the latter were beneficiaries and main users, the farmers and townspeople of Brecon had the satisfaction of seeing their coal prices cut by 60 per cent almost immediately after it opened.

You will observe during your stroll the essential moving parts of most canals: the lock, for example, is designed to allow the canal to run at different levels, compensating for changes in elevation of the land. Its operation is simple and you will see how it works as you pass. Another piece of canal furniture is the bridge. On this canal the bridges are all carefully numbered and are therefore convenient 'mileposts' for your journey. You will pass 21 bridges out of a total of 166 on the whole canal. Most are of stone, but there are intriguing wooden swing bridges used by farmers owning land on both sides of the waterway. A third feature, the aqueduct, is used to carry the canal over rivers and larger streams. This section offers one large aqueduct over the Usk and two small ones over tributaries. Culverts suffice to allow smaller streams to flow under the canal. It is impossible to get lost on this section. The level path makes for easy walking and the footing is excellent.

Talybont-on-Usk

NORTHWEST—Leave the B4558 in Talybont at the White Hart Inn and go through the inn yard to the canal towpath. Go R (NW) on the towpath. The canal immediately crosses the Afon Caerfanell by an aqueduct. Some 20yd beyond, the road to Aber village, the Talybont Reservoir and Pontsticill crosses the canal by a lift bridge (no 146). Since the bridge carries heavy traffic it is larger than the others you will encounter. Bridge no 150 is 1 mile from Talybont. Beyond it the river comes in view. At Bridge no 152 the remains of Penkelly Castle can be seen on the opposite bank. At Bridge no 153 the B4558 crosses the canal by the Royal Oak Hotel (refreshments available here) in the hamlet of Pencelli. Bridge no 157 is 3 miles from Talybont. The B4558 crosses the canal again at Bridge no 158. You are now at about the midpoint of your short journey. If it is lunchtime and you have not brought a packed lunch, you might think of digressing to the White Swan Inn at Llanfrynach. If so, go $\frac{1}{3}$ mile W on the B4558 and L at the first T-junction for $\frac{1}{3}$ mile to the inn. After lunch you may either return to the canal the way you came or reach the canal by a side road and B4558 N from the inn, adding a total of $\frac{3}{4}$ mile to your walk. If you return to the canal at Bridge no 158, look behind you soon for a good view of the Beacons. At Bridge no 161 the towpath changes banks so you have to cross the bridge. Just beyond, you cross the Usk on a stone aqueduct and the canal swings L along the river and passes under the B4558 for the third time (5 miles, Bridge no 162).

The only lock on this section of the canal is just ahead. At 6 miles you pass under the A40, and the B4601 runs close by the canal. By Bridge no 165 (7 miles) the evidence of approaching Aberhonddu (Brecon) grows stronger with each step. At the last bridge (no 166), cross to the N bank and to a road, Richway, running a short distance to Watton Street (B4601). Go L for the town centre.

SOUTHEAST—From the junction of the B4601 and B4602 (Watton Street and Free Street) in Brecon, walk E on Watton Street about $\frac{1}{4}$ mile to Richway and go R a short distance to the canal. Cross to the S bank and take the towpath SE to Talybont. The approximate distances are: Bridges no 163 2 miles, no 158 4 miles, no 155 5 miles, no 151 6 miles, no 148 7 miles.

PEMBROKESHIRE COAST PATH NORTH South Wales

51¼ miles (82·5km) 4 days

Section	Distance	Overnight Points
1	8m (13km)	Trefin (Trevine) – St Nicholas
2	14½m (23.25km)	St Nicholas – Goodwick
3	13¾m (22.25km)	Goodwick – Trefdraeth (Newport)
3a	8m (13km)	Goodwick – Dinas
3b	7½m (12km)	Dinas – Trefdraeth (Newport)
4	15m (24km)	Trefdraeth (Newport) – Llandudoch (St Dogmaels)
4a	9m (14.5km)	Trefdraeth (Newport) – Trewyddel (Moylgrove)
4b	8m (13km)	Trewyddel (Moylgrove) – Llandudoch (St Dogmaels)

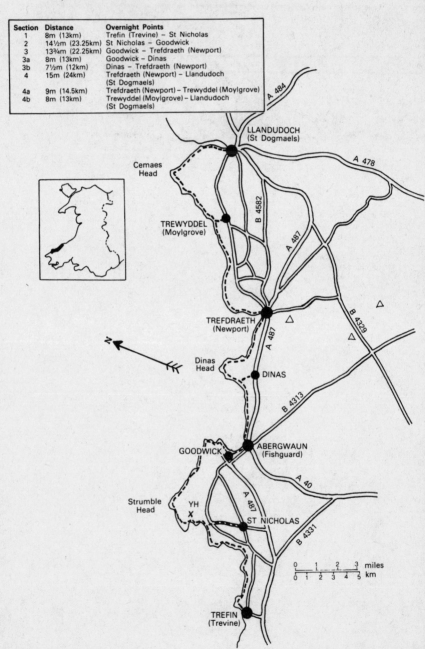

ACCOMMODATION
(Goodwick/Abergwaun (Fishguard) have more than 2 hotels listed)

Trefin	Cranog (GH) tel (03483) 392
(Trevine)	The Binchurn (F) (1m S on A487) tel (03483) 264
	Commerce House (GH) tel (03483) 372
St Nicholas	New Mill Farm (GH) tel (03485) 637
	Morawel (PH) tel (03485) 292
	Treseissyllt (F) tel (03485) 205
Dinas	Glanhelgy (GH) tel (03486) 369
	Clydfan (GH) Tel (03486) 202
	Cilwenen Hill (GH) tel (03486) 239
	The Glan (H) tel (03486) 309
Trefdraeth	Golden Lion Inn tel (0239) 820321
(Newport)	Llwyngwair Manor (H) tel (0239) 820498
	Sunnymeade, Parrog (GH) tel (0239) 820301
Trewyddel	Old Vicarage (GH) tel (0239) 231
(Moylgrove)	Penrallt Ceibwr (F) tel (0239) 217
	Glan-yr-afon (F) tel (023986) 686
Llandudoch	Commercial Hotel tel (0239) 614178
(St Dogmaels)	Glanteify (GH) tel (0239) 612353
	Webley Hotel, Poppit Sands tel (0239) 612085

PUBLIC TRANSPORT
Trefin (Trevine) bus (Richards) Fishguard 3 r/t dly Mon–Sat
St Nicholas bus (Richards) Fishguard 2 r/t Thurs
Goodwick train (British Rail) Haverfordwest, London 2 r/t dly, bus (Richards) Haverfordwest,
  Fishguard freq service Mon–Sat
Abergwaun (Fishguard) bus (Richards) Haverfordwest freq service Mon–Sat
Dinas bus (Richards) Cardigan, Fishguard 6 r/t dly Mon–Sat
Trefdraeth (Newport) bus (Richards) Cardigan, Fishguard 6 r/t dly Mon–Sat
Trewyddel (Moylgrove) bus (Richards) Cardigan 1 r/t Tues, 2 r/t Sat
Llandudoch (St Dogmaels) bus (Richards) Cardigan 6 r/t dly Mon–Sat

---

To give you a taste of coast walking, we have included part of the official long-distance path that runs for 180 miles along the west and south coasts of Pembrokeshire. We chose the northern quarter because, in general, it is wilder, more rugged and lonelier than the rest of that Path. Our memory of it is one of the sea, high cliffs, surf crashing on rocks far below, seabirds by the thousand, wheeling, crying, nesting, raiding, an occasional seal basking or fishing. In spite of being farmland right to the cliff edge, you will feel alone and miles from civilisation. Even a tractor ploughing, with a hundred gulls feeding in its wake, seems an object from another time and place. Your attention is seaward, downward or ahead as the next stretch of unknown land unfolds. There are four-footed animals sharing the path with you but you will rarely see them as they are nocturnal. Fox dens and badger setts line the way in places, with fresh earth, beaten trackways and droppings testifying to their presence.

You will have magnificent views at all times but the headlands particularly afford long views of the coastline. The flashing light of

43

Strumble Head will be a landmark seen from the northern half of the Walk. And, like clockwork, the white form of the Irish steamer will be seen along the entire length of the Walk, ploughing the water regularly twice a day. Most of the overnight points are very quiet villages where a stroll in the evening is the principal occupation. Even the town of Abergwaun (Fishguard) is only bustling by comparison.

We give this as a four-day walk and a fit walker can do it easily in that time. We have, however, broken two of the longer walks into two sections each, not just to make it easier but to give more time for bird-watching and viewing the ancient sites along the route. The way is carefully marked and it is impossible to mislay the Path other than momentarily. We therefore give instructions for one direction only. The footing is good to excellent all the way. The officials of the Pembroke-shire Coast National Park, who maintain the Path, have installed steps on the steepest slopes and filled or spanned almost all of the wet patches. There are still a lot of ups and downs, however, and it is not quite the stroll it sounds.

crossing in style

MAPS—We recommend both the 1:50,000 series Ordnance Survey maps and the Coast Path Cards (CPC) of the Pembrokeshire Coast National Park which are strip maps of sections of the Coast Path. Both are adequate but the CPCs are considerably less expensive (you will need 3 CPCs at 15p each or 2 OS maps at £2.40 each, at 1983 prices). You can order the CPCs (nos 8, 9 & 10) from: Pembrokeshire Coast National Park, Haverfordwest SA61 1QZ, and telephone for prices to (0437) 3131 ext 76. ·

OVERNIGHT POINTS—**Trefin (Trevine)** is a coastal village once the home of innumerable 'Cape Horners'. It was the birthplace of the Archdruid Trefin. Bishop David Martin built an episcopal palace here but no traces of it now remain. **St Nicholas** is a tiny village a mile or so from the sea. It boasts a church, chapel and a village shop but little else. **Goodwick** is a mile west of Abergwaun (Fishguard) across the Goodwick Sands, a smaller twin of the larger town. Once a fishing village, the building of a breakwater in Fishguard Bay and the blasting of the cliffs for a terminus for transatlantic steamers in 1906 changed its character. The transatlantic trade did not flourish and it is now the port for the Irish ferry. **Abergwaun's (Fishguard's)** main claim to fame lies in history. The last invasion of Britain took place in 1797 when a motley army of French troops and convicts landed to the west at Carreg Wasted (on your route between Goodwick and St Nicholas). They pillaged the farms near Goodwick for two days and surrendered at Goodwick Sands on the third. The surrender document was signed at the Royal Oak Inn, which is still in use in the town square. Some 30 years earlier, during the American War of Independence, John Paul Jones, the 'Father of the American Navy' seized a Goodwick ship off the bay and fired warning shots into Fishguard, demanding the ship's ransom, which was handed over. The lower town, at the mouth of the Gwaun, has an old harbour. The ruins of a fort dating from the time of the Napoleonic Wars are on the harbour's east headland. There is a marine walk that goes along the west shore. **Trefdraeth (Newport)** is an ancient town on the Afon Nyfer. The ruins of a Norman castle, built in 1195 by the Marcher Lord of Cemaes, is now incorporated into a guest house (Llwyngwair). The thirteenth-century church of St Mary, rebuilt in 1879, still has its original west tower. A 12ft early Christian cross-inscribed stone stands by the tower. Overlooking the town 1 mile south is Carn Igli (hill of angels) where there is an Iron Age fort and the remains of hut circles. The 33 Stonehenge dolerite bluestones were quarried and transported from here. **Dinas** is a village along the A487. A standing stone (The Lady Stone) and an Iron Age fort are east of the village (ask for directions locally). **Trewyddel (Moylgrove)** is a village on the Afon Ceibr 1 mile from the coast. It is named after Matilda, the wife of a Lord of Cemaes. There is a chalybeate well (Ffynnon Alwm), the waters of which are said to be inferior only to Tunbridge Wells'. **Llandudoch (St Dogmaels)** is an old fishing village on the west shore of the Teifi estuary. Its buildings are notable for their light and dark brown stone. There are extensive ruins of a twelfth-century Benedictine abbey in the vicarage grounds of the nineteenth-century parish church of St Thomas. There are ancient stone pillars in the church: the sixth-century Sagranus Stone, with both Latin and Ogham inscriptions, and one dating from the ninth or tenth century. The former enabled scholars to decipher Ogham, the early goidelic Irish alphabet.

1 TREFIN (TREVINE)–ST NICHOLAS
8 miles (13km) OS 157 or CPC no 8

This is a good introduction to the Coast Path since you will experience a sample of what the Path has to offer—mostly cliff-edge walking with a few beaches, usually only reached from the sea or by dangerous near vertical paths. Like all of this Walk, it is a lonely coast; yet it has known much human activity. You will pass a Bronze Age cromlech dating back to 3000 BC, once the burial chamber of a chieftain, and a promontory fort of the Iron Age. The medieval period is represented by the ruins of an old mill, and the more recent past, the beginnings of the Industrial Revolution, by a lime kiln, by the mill which operated into that period and by a harbour that once was the home port for coastal traders.

The basic occupation of the area has always been agriculture, on which all these other activities were grafted and that remains true today. Inland are low, rolling cultivated fields and pastures. It is a fertile land, specialising in dairy farming and potato growing. At one point we were startled to see the reflection of what looked like a sheet of water where, according to our maps, none was supposed to be. Closer inspection showed it to be a field covered by clear plastic sheeting. That evening our farmer host explained it was a new way of getting a two-week start in the 'early potato' market. A machine feeds ribbons of plastic over the rows of potato seedlings, making instant small greenhouse tunnels. While expensive, it must pay for itself by top prices for the first new potatoes.

Trefin mill

NORTH—From the centre of Trefin (Trevine) walk W ½ mile on the road to a small bay, Aberfelin. Go R a few yards to the Coast Path at the ruins of Melin Tre-fin Mill. A plaque here tells the story of the mill's 500-year history in the area. Walk N on the Path, passing some ruined buildings above the bay. You will follow the cliffs faithfully to Abercastle. At one small bay a side path zigzags down to a tiny beach (Pwllwhiting). Beyond, a promontory juts into the sea, its narrow neck defended by the remains of double ditches and ramparts, vestiges of a classic Iron Age fort (Castell-coch). Before the promontory you may notice fissures on the seaward side of the path where the land has begun to

Carreg Samson

slip into the sea. In two places we noticed fissures on the landward side, comforting only in the evident slow pace of the landslip. Beyond the fort, the path edges close to sheer cliffs below which two small islands hug the shore. About $\frac{1}{4}$ mile after the path turns SE towards Abercastle, on your R in an open field about 250yd inland are the remains of the Carreg Samson cromlech (on Longhouse Farm). It is one large stone perched on stone arms, all of it uncovered by the erosion of 5000 years. There is a footpath to it (with a footpath sign) near Abercastle. We found it worth the digression. Shortly after the sign you reach the tiny hamlet and bay ($3\frac{1}{2}$ miles), passing a lime kiln and a partly buried upright cannon by the shore. Abercastle was once a busy small port, its ships going to Bristol and Liverpool.

Go along the waterfront and climb N to the cliff edge past the ruins of a granary. Your view out to sea is dominated by a large rocky island at the entrance to the bay. There are some large sea caves below. You soon cross a fence to cultivated fields, a welcome change from the usual route along the sea side of wall, fence or hedgerow. After a steep descent to a cove, cross the bridge over a stream and climb again, repeating the down and up process twice more before the two shingle beaches of Abermawr and Aberbach come into view. Of all the unlikely places, Abermawr was chosen in 1850 to be the terminus and port for a railway and work was done in the small valley leading to the bay. It is difficult to imagine ever choosing the site, much less developing it. How nice for ramblers that the project failed.

Abercastle

After descending to Abermawr and going along its shelf of pebble, climb up to a road at a small turning place ($6\frac{1}{2}$ miles). There is a white house here which was once the terminus of a telegraph cable laid to Ireland in 1883. Walk down the road away from the beach, passing the point L where the Coast Path continues N. Go inland $\frac{1}{2}$ mile to a T-junction, turn L and, after crossing a stream, take a side road R (sign here to Tregwynt Mill). Treseissyllt Farm is less than $\frac{1}{2}$ mile N. Just as the road turns R you go by the entrance to New Mill Farm and in a few yards you pass Tregwynt Mill (shop and mill open to the public). At the next T-junction go L for $\frac{1}{2}$ mile to a crossroads and L again to St Nicholas. Morawel PH is W of the village centre, on the road towards Treseissyllt.

St Nicholas

2 ST NICHOLAS-GOODWICK
$14\frac{1}{2}$ miles (23·25km) OS 157 or CPC no 8

This is a lovely long day filled with the exhilaration of cliff walking. In the unlikely event that the way grows dull, there are places of interest along the route. Coming north you will first pass the youth hostel at Pwllderi. High above and facing the sea, it must be the most dramatically sited hostel in Britain. Behind it towers the 200m high Garn-fawr, crowned by the remains of a fine Iron Age fort, unusual in having both drystone walling and earth bank and ditch defences. The best approach, if you want to visit the fort, is from the landward side. The next attraction is the lighthouse at Strumble Head, built on a small island in 1906. It is reached by a bridge except when heavy seas make the crossing too dangerous. At such times the staff cross on a breeches-buoy which you can see. The light can be visited on some afternoons. The final point of interest is Carreg Wasted where the landing for the last invasion of Britain took place. There is a stone pillar to commemorate the event, erected 100 years later. The landing must have been in the small bay just east of the point and we wondered why so difficult and isolated a place was chosen. Our later readings told us that the invasion party simply got lost (see p44).

48

Strumble Light

The way is easy to follow except when rounding the headland into Fishguard Bay where care needs to be taken if only to stay on the shortest route. The footing is poor to good.

NORTH—From St Nicholas village centre walk W $\frac{1}{2}$ mile towards the coast on a road and go N at a T-junction to Velindre Farm. Here a footpath sign leads you L $\frac{1}{2}$ mile across farmland to the Coast Path at Pwllcrochan. Go N along cliffs that gradually increase in height. This stretch of coast has abundant birdlife and there is a good chance that you will also see seals playing in the water or dozing on the tiny beaches. At Pwllderi ($3\frac{3}{4}$ miles from St Nicholas) you pass the youth hostel and Garnfawr. Beyond Pwllderi the fertile farmland inland is replaced by heather, bracken and rock, and your sense of isolation increases. You will be on the barren Pencaer Peninsula for the rest of the way to Goodwick.

The bay beyond Pwllderi has a dramatic set of rock-cut steps leading precipitously down a cliff to the shingle (private and dangerous). The next headland provides you with your first view of the lighthouse at Strumble Head and you pass it at $6\frac{1}{2}$ miles.

By the lighthouse the path joins the access road for several 100yd, leaving it near a Coast Guard post and passing seaward of the latter. You keep well above the sea until you descend to Porthsychan Bay, passing a path R and crossing a stream that plunges to the shingle in a small waterfall. Here is the only grassland of the day and you may share the way with friendly cows. The bay is the site of St Dogan's Chapel but there are no visible remains. The next place of interest is Carreg Wasted, the landing point for the last invasion of Britain (p44). Beyond the point

Lower Fishguard

49

you descend steeply into a ravine through a deciduous wood and climb steeply out again, the only place where we found the footing at all difficult. From here the path grows less exciting. You round the turn into Fishguard Bay on a broad shallow slope well back from the sea. The way here is less easily followed and some guesswork may be necessary. You should pass by the remains of a small forest, turn uphill by some garden allotments on the R and reach Harbour Village at a street running between houses high above the bay. Go SE on this street and follow it downhill. If you are staying at Fishguard Bay Hotel, watch for a gap in a stone wall L halfway down the hill, and go through to a path that zigzags down to the hotel. Otherwise, continue down to the main street of Goodwick. For Abergwaun (Fishguard), dog-leg L to a road running across Goodwick Sands. Abergwaun (Fishguard) is 1 mile away.

Going S, you will have to watch for the exit to St Nicholas. It is at Pwllcrochan, a sand and pebble beach with a footpath running inland to Velindre Farm.

3 GOODWICK–
TREFDRAETH (NEWPORT)
13¾ miles (22km) OS 145, 157 or CPC no 9

This is another enjoyable day on the cliff tops. It is the least isolated section of the Walk as you pass two popular beaches and a caravan site. The centrepiece is Dinas Head, or Dinas Island as people persist in calling it, although the low neck connecting it with the mainland has not been under water for thousands of years. It consists of one large farm, with cultivated fields resting on top of sheer cliffs and rocky ledges.

In rounding the Head you will be counting the bird sightings rather than the miles. The seabirds will vie for your attention with field and moorland birds and you will have to be of sterner stuff than we to resist the temptation to be constantly stopping to watch and listen. We found it took two hours to complete the short 1¾-mile circuit. We met a local birdwatcher who told us about a raven's nest which she had been keeping under observation for the past fortnight. When we came to the spot she described and searched below, we were rewarded with the sight of three fledglings on the nest. They were well feathered and almost ready to fly so that if we had been a day or so later we would have missed them.

The footing is good and the way generally either evident underfoot or well marked. There are several sections along the edges of cultivated fields which have been erased by farmers eager to put the last inch to the plough. Here your sense of direction will carry you through. We have subdivided the walk into two sections for those wanting a less hurried journey.

3a GOODWICK–DINAS
8 miles (13km) OS 145, 157 or CPC no 9

NORTH—From Goodwick cross Goodwick Sands, which is really a shingle beach with a road and promenade. At the hill up to Abergwaun (Fishguard), go up steps at the end of the promenade to the A40 and go L a short distance to the first road on the L. Pass in front of a line of houses to a path (Marine Walk) that follows the coastline. Take the lower of any forks. You have a good view of the fort on the opposite headland and of the lower town and harbour. After the second shelter, take a dirt and grass path L to Bank Terrace (a road). Go L at its end down to the seawall and R along the wall to the A487. Go N across the bridge over the Afon Gwaum and uphill to an opening in a stone wall L (take great care crossing a narrow section of the main road in the lower town). A path runs R from the opening to the fort. The fort (*c*1800) is a modest one, with three rusting cannons facing outward and a ruined powder magazine (see p45). Go N from the fort on the Coast Path through rough moorland and low cliffs to a caravan site (3½ miles). Pick up the Path on the other side of the site (you may have to cast about for it) and continue N, sometimes along the edge of cultivated fields, to a lane. Go L down to the little bay of Hescwm (5 miles). Either jump the small stream to the shingle or go upstream on a path to a footbridge and return. Cross the shingle to the path and go on N to Pwllgwaelod (7 miles), the W bay at Dinas Head. There is a café here for refreshment. For Dinas village go R on the road 1 mile to the A487. The village is scattered along the A487.

rounding Dinas Head

51

3b DINAS–TREFDRAETH (NEWPORT)
7½ miles (12km) OS 145, CPC no 9

NORTH—Retrace your steps from Dinas to the bay of Pwllgwaelod and take the Coast Path around Dinas Head. The path is an easy but steady climb to the highest point of the Head (142m) and then a more varied downhill slope to the beach at Cwm-yr-eglwys. There are good views, at first of Fishguard Bay and the distant Strumble Head lighthouse and, as you move past the highest point, of Trefdraeth (Newport) and the coast beyond. On the E side you will pass Needle Rock, on which only birds can settle. You end your circuit of the Head, after passing through a green tunnel of trees and shrubs, at Cwm-yr-eglwys (valley of the church) 2¾ miles from Dinas.

If you are walking from Goodwick to Trefdraeth (Newport) in one day, you can omit Dinas Head and walk across the neck, saving a mile but missing the interesting Head. If you elect to do so, walk to the N edge of the café grounds to a footpath sign and stile leading to a level path that goes E to Cwm-yr-eglwys.

By the beach at Cwm-yr-eglwys is the ruin of twelfth-century St Brynach's Church, destroyed in the great storm of 1859 in which 114 ships were lost. The name of St Brynach crops up in many stories of the area. Our favourite concerns St Brynach's Cross, standing in the churchyard of nearby Nevern village, where, it seems, the first cuckoo song each spring is sung from a perch on that stone. We have not before met a saint honoured in such a melodious manner, nor a bird with so long a memory. From the cwm go L uphill on a steep road opposite the entrance to the car park. Go L by Percy Penrgh Farm (signposted). The next 3 miles are around small headlands on the cliff tops, making descents to two small coves, then climbing up to do it all again.

As you turn into the wide Nevern estuary, you will see Trefdraeth sands spread before you if it is low tide. Then you will have much to watch—horses being ridden over the sands and adults and children engaged in digging, wading and boating. Your path squeezes between houses and the estuary and you come out on the stone pier at Parrog. Go past the public toilets, up the road a short way and pick up the Path going L (unmarked but well trodden). You skirt the marsh and come out at a bridge. Trefdraeth is to the R. If you are staying at Parrog do not take this path but continue up the road from the pier to your lodgings.

4 TREFDRAETH (NEWPORT)–LLANDUDOCH (ST DOGMAELS)
15 miles (24km) OS 145 or CPC no 10

This most northerly leg of the Walk goes through scenery generally more remote and wilder than the sections to the south. Although for part of it you pass along the usual patchwork fields edged by hedgerows and filled with sheep, cattle or corn, there are long stretches where you will be walking through rough grass, gorse and heather 100 to 150m above the sea (the highest point of the Coast Path is here at 171m).

The two end points boast the best stretches of sandy beach and dunes on this Walk, and there are enough steep ups and downs along the way to provide a pleasant exertion for even the fittest leg muscles. While the cliffs along the whole Walk afford the study of geological processes, this section seems to display the most spectacular patterns. The rocks of the cliffsides are bent, pressed and folded into intricate forms, with rising columns, both perpendicular and slanting, alternating with horizontal serpentine stripes of different colours: the dead diagrams of geology textbooks brought alive in the field.

One spot remains particularly in our memory; the wild little bay of Pwllygranant where a stream comes down a steep, narrow gorge in a series of small waterfalls and pools. We were there in early spring and found its edges covered with a new ruffle of bright green and white scurvy-grass. In the hot summer you will be tempted to dabble in the pools or swim in the sea at the stream's foot. We were content with its visual charms.

Again, for a more leisurely expedition with time along the way, you can take two days over the Walk, stopping the night at Trewyddel (Moylgrove). The detailed description of the route is therefore divided into two parts. The footing is generally good to excellent, with steps on the steeper slopes. The way is straightforward.

4a TREFDRAETH (NEWPORT)– TREWYDDEL (MOYLGROVE)
9 miles (14·5km) OS 145 or CPC no 10

NORTH—Walk N from Trefdraeth (Newport) on a road going L from the A487, E of the Golden Lion Inn, cross the Afon Nyfer, and beyond the bridge go L on the signposted Coast Path. This takes you along the estuary and then inland of the golf course to a road running down to Newport Sands. The Path goes R before the shore but, if it is not high tide, we recommend going N along the sands under the cliffs, exploring the caves and sealife left behind by the tide. The sands end at Pen Pistyl, a tiny waterfall, and you must scramble up beside it to the Path. Go L and climb along the cliff edge to Morfa Head, one of the highest points on the Path. Your way is very near the edge, with the sea breaking a giddy distance below. Descend and immediately climb again to a short section of high, reasonably level cliff; and then go by downs and ups, most conveniently stepped, to the promontory of Carregysbar (7 miles). Descend to Pwll-y-Wrach or the Witches' Cauldron, a collapsed cave into which the sea surges. You will cross the arch under which the tide floods and hear the music of the water beneath your feet. A further ½ mile N you reach a road at Ceibwr Bay. Go L on the road 1 mile to Trewyddel (Moylgrove).

4b TREWYDDEL (MOYLGROVE)-LLANDUDOCH (ST DOGMAELS)

8 miles (13km) OS 145 or CPC no 10

NORTH—Retrace your steps to Ceibwr Bay. The Coast Path goes R (N) off the road and you cross an estuary on a footbridge. From the bridge climb to a farm lane and go away from the cliff edge to a path around a farmhouse, turning L beyond it to regain the coast. Be sure to follow this well-marked loop and do not try to walk on the cliff tops before this as the cliff edges here are subject to severe erosion and are not safe.

You will have farmland on your R for the next $1\frac{1}{2}$ miles until you descend to sea level at Pwllgranant Bay. Beyond, you zigzag steeply back to the cliff tops. Inland, the farms disappear and you will be on moorland until Cemaes Head. Before the Head you will reach a signpost (1 mile to Allt-y-goed Farm) and beyond it a locked Coast Guard post. As you round the promontory you will have a good view of Poppit Sands and the Teifi estuary. On the opposite side of the estuary is the wildlife sanctuary of Cardigan Island. If you look back before turning E, you will see the light flashing on Strumble Head, a fitting farewell to your long walk. It is 14 miles away as the raven flies but 32 miles by the path.

At Allt-y-goed ($5\frac{1}{2}$ miles) go R through the farmyard. We had trouble getting through because a very large, very muddy, sow sprawled completely across the narrow way. From the farm a rough lane runs $1\frac{1}{2}$ miles down to Poppit Sands. Llandudoch (St Dogmaels) is $1\frac{1}{4}$ miles E by road. Some of the available accommodation is along this road.

on guard

WYE VALLEY WALK
Mid Wales
39½ miles (63·5km) 4 days

Section	Distance	Overnight Points
1	9¼m (15km)	Y Gelli (Hay-on-Wye) – Llyswen
2	11¾m (19km)	Llyswen – Llanfair ym Muallt (Builth Wells)
3	9m (14.5km)	Llanfair ym Muallt (Builth Wells) - Newbridge-on-Wye
4	9½m (15.25km)	Newbridge-on-Wye – Rhaiadr Gwy (Rhayader)

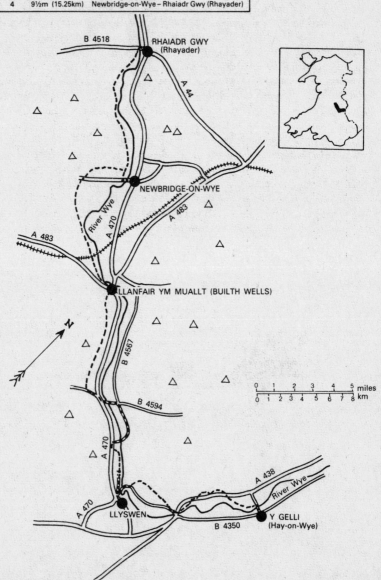

ACCOMMODATION
(except as noted below, overnight points have more than 2 hotels listed)

Llyswen   Lower Rhydness Farm tel (087485) 264
                                  The Boat Inn tel (087485) 359
Newbridge-on-Wye   New Inn tel (059789) 211
                                  Oaklands Bungalow (PH) tel (059789) 326

PUBLIC TRANSPORT
Y Gelli (Hay-on-Wye) bus (National Welsh) Brecon, Hereford 5 r/t dly Mon–Sat
Llyswen bus (TrawsCambria) Bangor–Cardiff 1 r/t dly, summer, 1 r/t Fri, Sat, Sun, Mon winter
Llanfair ym Muallt (Builth Wells) bus (TrawsCambria) Bangor–Cardiff 1 r/t dly, summer, 1 r/t Fri,
    Sat, Sun, Mon winter, bus (National Express) Cheltenham–Aberystwyth 1 r/t dly summer, 1r/t Fri, Sat,
    Sun, Mon winter
Newbridge-on-Wye bus (TrawsCambria) Bangor/Cardiff (as above)
Rhaiadr Gwy (Rhayader) bus (National Express) Cheltenham–Aberystwyth 1 r/t dly summer, 1 r/t Fri,
    Sat, Sun, Mon winter

This is a ramble for all seasons, displaying the rural beauty of the upper Wye Valley, with the broad river sometimes wandering leisurely through fertile fields and sometimes hurrying between high hills. The path divides its time impartially between the riverbank and the hillsides high above the river, never long enough on one kind of terrain to become tiresome. There is much birdlife—especially along the river. The way is mostly along footpaths, farm tracks and deserted country roads, although you occasionally risk short sections of busy major road. In spite of the closeness of habitation and the proximity of main roads, there is a satisfying sense of remoteness. Three of the five overnight points (Y Gelli (Hay-on-Wye), Llanfair ym Muallt (Builth Wells) and Rhaiadr Gwy (Rhayader)) are interesting small towns with plenty to do and see. The remaining two are quiet hamlets where an evening walk and a chat with the local inhabitants are the major attractions.

The route was established by the forward-looking Powys County Council and has been made possible by the co-operation of local farmers and landowners (remember your Countryside Manners, see p163). The way is well signposted at critical points by broad yellow arrows painted on fence posts, walls and telegraph poles, but you will still need the help of the OS maps.

OVERNIGHT POINTS—Y Gelli (Hay-on-Wye) is an attractive Welsh market town on the south bank of the Wye just inside the Anglo-Welsh border. It sits astride an easy passage between the two regions. Thus it has known the march of armies and enjoyed the movement of trade. The ruins of a thirteenth-century Norman castle occupy a hill in the centre of the town with a seventeenth-century Jacobean mansion (now gutted by fire) built against it. Below the castle are narrow winding streets with attractive houses and numerous shops. A small clocktower in the town square helps mark the passage of time. On Mondays there are fatstock sales—cattle, Clun and Kerry sheep and occasional horses and

ponies—in the Smithfield or cattle market by the river. A river walk
starts from St Mary's Church and runs to the Warren, a picnic and
swimming area. Part of the walk is on an old tramway from Brecon,
along which horse-drawn cars carried coal and passengers from 1816 until
1864 when it was superseded by the railway. To the visitor, the
outstanding feature of the town is the baker's dozen of secondhand
bookshops. It is claimed that the town is the second largest (London being
the largest) secondhand book centre in the world. **Llyswen** is a straggling

village on the Wye along the Builth Wells road. The name, meaning
White Court, is said to derive from a mansion built by the Welsh prince,
Roderick the Great. The mansion is long since gone and in its place is
Llangoed Castle, which was built at the turn of the century, and which
you pass on your way north of Llyswen. The village is reputed to be the
birthplace of Llewelyn the Last. At the south end is Y Dderw, farm
buildings of medieval origin. The bird sanctuary of Brechfa Pool, high
above the village and a short mile walk (see OS map), is a good place for
bird and valley viewing of an evening. **Llanfair ym Muallt** (Builth
Wells) began as a settlement around a Norman castle built on the mound
behind the Lion Hotel. The town grew in size and popularity in the
eighteenth century as a spa. Its two wells are not now in use. It is a busy
place one week in July when the Royal Welsh Agricultural Society holds
its annual show across the river at Llanelwedd. It is worth arranging your
walk for that time in order to enjoy the activities. Between the main
shopping street and the river is the Groe, a park with sports fields. Close to
its entrance is a grey stone chapel. The Market Hall (1877) by the eight-
arched bridge houses the Wyeside Art Centre. **Newbridge-on-Wye** is a
sleepy hamlet. An old drovers' pub is now an art gallery and craftmen's
workshop (Mid Wales House). An attractive old building worth noting is
the New Inn, so is the village church. Newbridge-on-Wye had its
moment in history when it was one of the centres of the Rebecca Riots of
1843. These were attacks by farmers on the newly erected toll gates which
were making the transport of farm produce more expensive at a time of
agricultural depression. The protesters called themselves 'Rebecca's
Daughters' because they carried out their attacks dressed as women with
blackened faces. **Rhaiadr Gwy (Rhayader)** means waterfall on the Wye
and refers to the falls now largely destroyed by the town bridge built in

1780. It is a small market town (cattle and sheep market on Wednesday) built at the intersection of two main roads. There are several old inns (Cwmdeuddwr and the Triangle) near each end of the bridge. In the angle between Church Street and West Street is a large mound, once the site of an early Norman castle. North of it is Waun Capel Park from which a bridge leads over the Wye to a riverside walk. Just below the town bridge, on the west bank, is a nicely sited green.

Y Gelli

1 Y GELLI (HAY-ON-WYE) – LLYSWEN
$9\frac{1}{4}$ miles (15km) 245ft (75m) OS 161

This is the most rural part of the Walk, with the Wye Valley at its widest and with the farmland spreading up the hillsides. One-third of your time will be spent along the river and the rest on paths and quiet roads through farmland well above the river. The paths along the river include stretches favoured by swans, herons and other waterbirds. We saw an armada of twenty swans, an impressive cloud of white, swimming in still water below Glasbury Bridge. Swans are seen everywhere in Britain and are as commonplace as their majestic beauty permits the use of that word; they are the most numerous of the *Cygninae* family and their proper name is the mute swan. This is not because they are truly mute, being able to make explosive or hissing noises, but because other swans, such as the winter-visiting Whooper and Bewick's swans, possess loud and resonant voices, the true swan song. The mute swan is extremely sociable and may be found in large groups except in the breeding season. The cygnet or

mute swan

young swan has a suit of grey and brown feathers; they were highly esteemed for the table in olden times, a habit almost unthinkable now as we cherish them for their ornamental grace. Be careful with these birds, however, if you encounter them out of water as they are powerful, and courageous and their beaks are formidable weapons. Retreat discreetly if they curve their necks and arch their wings over their backs.

You may see a gaggle of canoes above the Glasbury bridge, milling about like excited waterbeetles. It is a favourite launching spot. The experts will be impressive, the tyros entertaining. The way is not quite as well marked as the rest of the Walk but is easy to follow. The footing is good and mostly dry.

NORTH—From Y Gelli (Hay-on-Wye) cross the river Wye on the B4351 towards Clyro. Up the road $\frac{1}{4}$ mile go L through a gate just before a walled entrance to a tree-lined driveway (Wye Cliff). Keep close to the hedge on the R to the corner of the field; go over a stile and take the R fork along a garden wall. Near the stile is a stone in memory of Bill Barker 'who killed many salmon opposite this stone'. From the garden wall you will have a good view of the river. You may see canoeists running the small rapids here or going back upstream to try again. From the wall the path runs through a wood to a second stile and on to a third stile before coming out to open fields. Bear L past a house and follow the path along the river for about 2 miles until you reach the A438. Cross and go L a short distance to a steep track R, through a gate and on uphill through another gate by a stream. Take the next gate L into a field. Follow a hedge along the top of the field. You will have good views of the river valley below, with the town of Hay-on-Wye to the L and Glasbury and its bridge to the R. Beyond are the Black Mountains and their wooded foothills. Go through a gate at the end of the field to a track into a small wood, then through an orchard to a gate by Llowes Church. Either go L a few yards to the A438 and R or ahead through the churchyard to a road going R off the A438 (the Radnor Arms across the A438 for refreshments). If the church is open, stop for a visit. There is a 7ft seventh-century Celtic cross here which, legend has it, dropped from the apron of the giantess, Moll Walbee, while she was rebuilding Hay Castle in one night. The stone fell into her shoe and, finally tiring of the discomfort, she removed it and threw it over the Wye into the churchyard, a respectable 2-mile throw.

Take this side road off the A438 beyond the buildings in Llowes, and just past the last of several old farm buildings go L through a gate into a field, follow a fence on your R to its corner and then head uphill across the open slope slightly to the R of the fence line to an opening that leads into a bracken-covered field (the opening is well L of a large dead tree). Go along the lower part of this field to a dirt track going L to a farm and take the farm lane down to the A438. In the winter and spring, before the new bracken has grown, the way should be easy. However, in summer and autumn the bracken grows shoulder-high and the way may be difficult to force. We struggled into it on a hot September day and had to give up after several 100yd. If this happens to you, just go downhill a short distance to an open field, skirt its edge to a low stone wall and go over it to the dirt track already mentioned. The farm is L. Once on the A438 go R for $\frac{1}{3}$ mile to a footpath sign. Go L, cross an old unused section of the road and go through a gate into an open field by the river. Go R along the river for $\frac{1}{2}$ mile to steps leading up to Glasbury Bridge 5 miles from Hay-on-Wye, negotiating a series of kissing-gates on the way. The river here is a favourite place for starting canoe runs so you may have a show to watch. There are refreshment places at each end of the bridge.

From here go W on the B4350 for $\frac{1}{2}$ mile. Shortly after the Woodlands Outdoor Centre, take the last of three roads that go off R in rapid succession. It was marked in 1982 by a somewhat drunken and dilapidated sign to Skynlais. In $\frac{1}{4}$ mile take a L fork that goes in front of a white house and ends in its farmyard. Continue ahead through a gate on a track that winds between fences for about 1 mile to Cilgwyn Farm. The track is mostly green, with some mud and dirt depending on the weather, and it takes one sharp R turn about $\frac{1}{8}$ mile from Skynlais. From Cilgwyn take the farm lane L 1 mile to a T-junction by an adventure centre and go L to a second T-junction opposite Castle Farm. Go L past the entrance to Boughrood Castle to the B4350 and R to Boughrood Bridge over the Wye. Cross to the A470. Llyswen is $\frac{1}{4}$ mile to the L.

SOUTH—Walk N on the A470 from Llyswen and go R on the B4350. Take the second road L after the bridge. Opposite Castle Farm go R on a road signposted to Cornhill. Take the next road R by an adventure centre and walk about 1 mile to Cilgwyn Farm. Go into the farmyard and take a

water beetles

track E (yellow arrow) about 1 mile to Lower Skynlais Farm and a lane downhill to the B4350. Go L 1 mile to the A438 in Glasbury. Walk R towards the bridge over the river and take steps L just before the bridge to a path along the river. This leads back to the A438 (leave river when way is blocked by a thicket). Go R (N) $\frac{1}{3}$ mile to second road L (to Bry-yr-hydd Farm) and go through the farm to a track and then a path parallel to but high above the A438. When you reach a road go R to the A438 in Llowes and L 100yd to a path L up through an orchard and wood $\frac{1}{2}$ mile back to the A438. Dog-leg L to a path along the river to Wye Cliff and the B4351. Hay is $\frac{1}{4}$ mile to the R. The distances are: Cilgwyn Farm 2 miles, Glasbury $4\frac{1}{4}$ miles, Llowes $6\frac{1}{4}$ miles.

2 LLYSWEN–LLANFAIR YM MUALLT (BUILTH WELLS)
$11\frac{3}{4}$ miles (19km) 885ft (270m) OS 147

This section, at its southern end, offers the best bit of riverside rambling of the Walk. It is along a particularly secluded part of the river much favoured by fishermen and grey herons and you will be sure to see both. The grey heron is one of Britain's largest birds. It grows to 3ft in height with a wing span to 6ft. It is shy and will fly up ahead of you, its head sunk between its shoulders and its wings beating slowly but powerfully. Since it often stands motionless and its colour blends so well with the background, you may only notice it when it flies up. It generally nests in trees in flocks but we looked in vain for heronries, which are generally easily distinguished by the many untidy nests of sticks or, late in the day, by the resident crowd of herons. The riverbank here offers stretches of large trees, open meadows, even an old graveyard replete with ancient funereal yews casting their gloomy shade.

The remainder of the section is away from the river on high ground, mostly moorland but with some woodland. The river and its immediate valley are constantly in view and continue to dominate the scene. The way is well marked, the footing good to excellent.

grey heron

NORTH — Walk N $\frac{1}{4}$ mile on the A470 from Llyswen to the B4350. Go R a few yards to a road L just before Boughrood Bridge. This road runs along the river for about $\frac{1}{4}$ mile and ends at a water pumping station. You continue along the river by paths for about 2 miles, the leisurely highlight of the day's ramble. You will pass two graves in a grove of ancient yews, a standing stone alone in a cultivated field, open woods of giant beeches and the vast pile of Llangoed Castle. Almost too soon your way is barred by the Scithwen Brook and you must go L to the A470 by an old mill. Go R $\frac{1}{8}$ mile on the A470 to the first road R and cross the Wye on the narrow Llanstephan suspension bridge, scarcely wide enough for one car. Continue on the road to a junction and go L parallel to the river for 2 miles on a road built on an abandoned railway bed. This is a roadside nature reserve and it has an abundance of flowering plants. You will cross over a road that leads L to Erwood Bridge. Scramble down the bank to it and cross the bridge to the A470, 5 miles from Llyswen. Dog-leg L to a lane W, marked Twmpa on the map and once an old drover's road. Go uphill about $\frac{1}{2}$ mile to a path R just below a roadside landfill (yellow arrow on pole here). The path goes gently downhill on grass. At a gate dog-leg L uphill for a short distance, and then go R and cross a small stream, the Fernant, by a plank bridge to a lane, 7 miles from Llyswen. Go L on the lane, steeply uphill at first and then at a gentler gradient, for 1 mile to a farm track L. Take it a short distance to a gate and go R on a path uphill. You will have good views of the river valley and the Aberedw Rocks across the river. Follow the path along a fence L. Just before a second gate take a track R (N) and follow it on smooth turf and bracken for $1\frac{1}{2}$ miles through several gates. The track is distinct and there are occasional markers of yellow paper or painted yellow arrows. You can see Llanfair ym Muallt (Builth Wells) far ahead. The track turns downhill and passes a large mound. Go through a gate by the mound and follow a fence for a short distance to a second gate. Go L in front of it and along a field edge to a third gate and a farm track beyond. Follow the track to a lane (10 miles) and go L $\frac{1}{8}$ mile until the lane goes sharp L. Take a track ahead downhill to a footbridge over the Afon Duhonw. Cross to a road going steeply uphill and follow it for 1 mile to Llanfair ym Muallt (Builth Wells).

Boughrood Bridge

SOUTH—From the carpark in Llanfair ym Muallt (Builth Wells) go S on the A470 to Castle Street. Turn R to Castle Mound and take the R fork, staying beside the Mound. Take the second fork L (Newry Street) and continue S on it for 1 mile to a ford and bridge over the Duhonw. Cross to a track SE uphill past a house R to a lane. Go L (SE) on the lane for $\frac{1}{8}$ mile, and take the first dirt track R uphill past the sign 'Pant-y-byllau'. When the track turns sharp R towards a farmhouse, continue straight ahead up through a gate. Follow a grassy track uphill along a fence on the L. At the top of the field the track turns R, you pass a large mound R and go through a gate on the L. Follow the track S uphill and then mostly on a contour along the E side of Pant-y-llyn Hill and Banc-y-Celyn for $1\frac{1}{2}$ miles. When the track divides, go L downhill to a gate and farm lane which leads in a few yards to a road. Go R for 1 mile. A few yards past a steep descent and farm, take a track sharp R, descend and cross a small stream (Fernant) on a plank bridge to a grassy track S. Go through several gates (track direction will be marked by arrows) and go gently up and downhill for $\frac{1}{2}$ mile to a road. Go L downhill for $\frac{1}{2}$ mile, cross the A470 and take Erwood Bridge across the Wye. Several 100yd beyond the bridge the road goes through an underpass. Scramble up the side of the underpass to the road above and go S (R). Take the first road R and recross the river on Llanstephan suspension bridge to the A470. Go L past an old mill R and bridge over Scithwen Brook. Just beyond the bridge go L through a gate to a field by the river. Take a path S along the river for 2 miles to a road running to the B4350. Dog-leg R to the A470. Llyswen is $\frac{1}{4}$ mile L (S) on the A470. Distances are, by bridges: Duhonw 1 mile, Fernant $4\frac{3}{4}$ miles, Erwood $6\frac{1}{4}$ miles, Llanstephan $8\frac{1}{2}$ miles.

3 LLANFAIR YM MUALLT (BUILTH WELLS) – NEWBRIDGE-ON-WYE

9 miles (14·5km) 555ft (170m) OS 147

This section continues the combination of riverbank and high ground walking of section 2. It makes a wide sweep away from the river, this time into high farmland and oak woods. These woods add a rich sample of woodland birds to your, by now familiar, collection of waterbird sightings. The way is distinguished by Penddol Rocks, a series of rocky rapids in the river, magnificent if the river is high. Halfway, you pass a small sixteenth-century barn-type church. There will be views from the high ground of Newbridge-on-Wye, Llandrindod Wells and the hills beyond. The way is well marked and easy to follow. The footing varies from boggy bits along the river to firm turf and the tarmac of small roads.

NORTH—From the riverside car park in Llanfair ym Muallt, walk NW for ½ mile along the SW bank of the Wye on recreation fields to Afon Irfon, and go L to a path which crosses the Irfon by a suspension bridge. Cross and turn R through a gate back to the Wye and continue NW along the riverside. There is boggy land here and it is a favourite haunt of herons. Further on you will pass the rapids at Penddol Rocks. At 1¾ miles you pass under a railway bridge. Beyond, the path moves away from the river and you go over several stiles and through various gates, through woods and over another stile to a road. Go R. Beyond the turning for Dolyrerw Farm the road becomes a track and then a path along the river.

blackthorn

The path leaves the river at a stile and you climb through woods to a field and cross diagonally uphill to its far corner. Go through a gap in the hedgerow to a road. Go R for about 2 miles to the B4358, passing a road R at ½ mile. Go R on the B4358 to the first road L (6 miles). This leads past a village hall, several ruined cottages and the tiny Llanfihangel Brynpabuan Church. At ¼ mile from the B4358 look for farm track R. You go downhill a short distance on it. As you near the Afon Hirnant, look for an unmarked track R that crosses the stream. Take it and it will lead you by woods and fields through a variety of gates along the SE side of Banc Craigol hill to a farm lane. You will have extensive views of the Wye

Valley along the way. At a barn go R on a green track $\frac{1}{4}$ mile to Penrhiw Farm. Turn sharp L at the farm, keeping on the farm lane. In $\frac{1}{2}$ mile you reach Llethr Farm and soon pass the University of Wales Institute of Science and Technology Field Centre (marked Llysdinam on the OS map) and in another $\frac{1}{2}$ mile reach a T-junction. Go R for $\frac{1}{3}$ mile downhill to the B4358. Newbridge-on-Wye is $\frac{1}{4}$ mile to the L.

SOUTH—Go W $\frac{1}{4}$ mile on the B4358 from Newbridge-on-Wye and take the first road R (N) after crossing the Wye. Climb $\frac{1}{3}$ mile and take the first road L for $\frac{1}{2}$ mile to a farm (Llethr Farm). Go straight ahead past a barn, through a gate and take a track $\frac{1}{2}$ mile to a second farm. Immediately before the farm go R on a faint track downhill (arrow here on a telegraph pole), cross Eslyn Brook on a footbridge to a gate and field beyond. Follow yellow arrows for about 1 mile across fields and by tracks, first NW and then SW under Banc Craigol. The complicated route, made easy by the yellow arrows, ends at a farm track shortly after you cross Hirnant Brook. Go S to a road and L to the B4358. Go R to the first road L (S) and follow it for 2 miles, passing a road L on the way. About $\frac{1}{4}$ mile after passing the small house of Goytre, go L through an opening in a hedgerow (well marked) and cross a field diagonally R to its bottom far corner, picking up a path descending through woods toward the Wye. Cross a stile to a path by the river. The path becomes a track and you pass small bungalows and the entrance to Dolyerw Farm on the L. In $\frac{1}{2}$ mile, as the track approaches a wood, go over a stile L into the wood and follow a path by stiles and gates. You pass under a railway bridge over the Wye and continue along the Wye until you reach the Afon Irfon. Turn R uphill along this stream to a gate and suspension footbridge over the stream. Cross and go L back to the Wye and walk on playing fields into Llanfair ym Muallt (Builth Wells). The distances are: Hirnant Brook $2\frac{1}{2}$ miles, Goytre Farm 5 miles, railway bridge 7 miles.

4 NEWBRIDGE-ON-WYE – RHAIADR GWY (RHAYADER)

9½ miles (15·25km) 740ft (225m) OS 147

early Watt

The Wye passes through high hills on this section; the route takes to the hill slopes and even climbs over a 210m summit. You will therefore have good views, and the way is constantly changing. You come off the hills to find restful benches beside a placid section of the river, and pass from country roads to tracks and paths, from riverside to hillside and back. You will go past wealthy James Watt's magnificent country estate but may remember him better as a poor boy tending a primitive steam engine and dreaming of its improvement: a dream that was fulfilled and helped to launch the Industrial Revolution.

The day we walked into Rhaiadr Gwy we passed a sloping field in which sheepdog trials were being held. Naturally, we stopped to watch the shepherds directing their dogs. It seemed just short of uncanny the way the dogs responded both to the voice and whistle commands of their owners and countered the maddening vagaries of the woolly-minded sheep, driving them through multiple gates into the final pen. We enjoyed tea in bone china cups, delivered from a dilapidated caravan by smiling ladies, and talked with waiting contestants who took pity on our abysmal ignorance about sheepdog life and patiently dispelled some of it.

The way is well marked; the footing good to excellent.

dog trial?

NORTH—Go W for $\frac{1}{4}$ mile on the B4358 from Newbridge-on-Wye and take the first road R (N) after crossing the Wye. In $1\frac{1}{4}$ miles go R at a crossroad and in $\frac{1}{4}$ mile go R again. This leads downhill, and in $\frac{3}{4}$ mile you go L over a little stone bridge near an abandoned railway line to a green track, $2\frac{1}{2}$ miles from Newbridge. Take this track N over open country for 2 miles to a farm. There are fine views NE across the Wye of Rhiw Gwraidd hill, under it Doldowlod House, built by James Watt, and Dol-y-fan Hill to the R. From the farm take a road N to Llanwrthwl (6 miles) (no shops or public houses). In the village go L at the chapel and take the first road R, marked to Elan village and at next fork go sharp R. In a short distance, just beyond the entrance to the first house R (Glan-rhos), take a rough farm track L through a gate and climb moderately steeply 200m, passing R of a farm house and farm buildings at the top of the rise. Continue ahead on the level for $\frac{1}{8}$ mile to a fork and go R downhill to a road. On the way down you will have good views of Gwastedyn Hill and its busy quarry NW across the river. To the N you will see the buildings of Rhaiadr Gwy and below you will see the next section of your route. Go R on the road to the river and L on a path along the river (comfortable benches here) to a suspension bridge over the Afon Elan (8 miles). The climb over Cefn may be avoided if the weather is miserable by continuing N on the road along the river from Glan-rhos. From the suspension bridge go R to a farm track running N to a farm and continue N on a road. After you pass under a railway bridge go L on a farm lane (to Glan Elan). Pass the farm without going under the railway to a track running N. In $\frac{1}{2}$ mile you join a road and continue N for another $\frac{1}{2}$ mile to the B4518 on the outskirts of Rhaiadr Gwy. The town centre is to the R.

Rhaiadr Gwy

SOUTH—Walk W on the B4518 from the clocktower in Rhaiadr Gwy, cross the Wye and take the first road L (S). Go down past a playing field and river on the L (look back at old bridge over the Wye) and climb to a fork. Take the R fork straight ahead on a gravel and then grass track and turn L and go parallel to an abandoned railway line (do not go under it here) on a farm lane to a road. Go R and pass under the railway to the Glyn farmyard. Take a track S near the river to the field by the Afon Elan and go R upstream a few yards to a suspension bridge. Cross and go L to

the Wye and a path S to a road. Go R uphill, and opposite the first house take a rocky track L and climb steeply through bracken to Bwlch-coch. It is an obvious pony-trekking track and you will pass two old houses on the R. At the top of the rise the track joins another track. Go L to the farm lane, past the Cefn Farm and descend steeply to a road. Note the beautiful views that Cefn commands to the S and W before you descend. Go R for a short distance to a T-junction and go L and then L again into Llanwrthwl. Turn R by the chapel in the village to a road running S along the river. The road ends at a farm and you continue SE 2 miles on a track that ends at a small stone bridge. Cross to a road and go R uphill to a T-junction. Go L to a crossroads and L again for $1\frac{1}{4}$ miles to the B4358. Newbridge-on-Wye is $\frac{1}{4}$ mile to the L. The distances are: Afon Elan $1\frac{1}{2}$ miles, Llanwrthwl $3\frac{1}{2}$ miles, stone bridge 7 miles.

MAWDDWY WALK
Mid Wales
29½ miles (47·5km) 3 days

Section	Distance	Overnight Points
1	6½m (10.5km)	Tywyn – Corris via Talyllyn Railway
2	12m (19.25km)	Corris – Dinas Mawddwy
3	11m (17.75km)	Dinas Mawddwy – Bala via Bala Lake Railway
3a	12m (19.25km)	Dinas Mawddwy – Bala (lower level alternative)

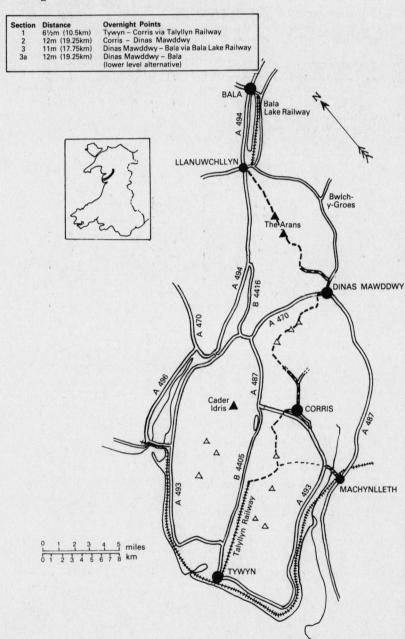

Corris	Braich Goch Hotel tel (0654) 229
	Foel Friog (F) tel (0654) 637
	Rhianfa (PH) (Corris Uchaf) tel (0654) 283
Dinas Mawddwy	Red Lion Hotel tel (06504) 247/260
	Buckley Arms Hotel tel (06504) 261
	Tawelfan (PH) tel (06504) 371
	Tremynfa (PH) tel (06504) 240
Llanuwchllyn	Wenddu (F) tel (06784) 277
	Bryn Farm tel (06784) 284

PUBLIC TRANSPORT

Tywyn train (British Rail) Machynlleth, London freq service Mon–Sat, bus (Crosville) Dolgellau, Barmouth freq service Mon–Sat, train (Talyllyn) Nant Gwernol late Mar–late July, Sept, 2 r/t dly; late July–Aug, 6 r/t dly

Corris bus (Crosville) Dolgellau, Machynlleth 4 r/t dly Mon–Sat

Dinas Mawddwy bus (Crosville) Machynlleth 2 r/t dly Mon–Sat

Llanuwchllyn bus (Crosville) Bala, Llangollen, Wrexham 4 r/t dly, train (Bala Lake Railway) Bala mid April–mid June 4 r/t dly; mid June–July 6 r/t dly; Aug 9 r/t dly

Bala bus (Crosville) Llangollen, Wrexham 4 r/t dly

This Walk is unique in combining two narrow-gauge railways to start and end a 3 day ramble over high ridges between the coast and Bala Lake. It includes the full length of the Arans which has the highest peak south of Snowdonia. The overnight points of Corris and Dinas Mawddwy are true mountain villages, nestling in narrow valleys which are hemmed in on all sides by mountains and high hills.

We include two of the 'Little Railways' of Wales mostly because we love railways, especially steam-driven trains. Moreover, there are practical advantages. It makes the Walk accessible by British Rail and, while buses provide a flexible, less costly mode of travel, trains are more comfortable and the view of the passing scene is unbeatable. For those seasons or times when the narrow-gauge railways do not run, you can start at Machynlleth by using part of the Snowdonia Walk and end at Llanuwchllyn instead of Bala.

These two narrow-gauge railways and the six others in Wales now rank with Snowdon and the Welsh castles as popular tourist attractions. Developed for the slate industry, the railways began to decline as the sale of slate diminished. Their existence today is owed to volunteer groups who took over and re-established a number of them with such success that commercial enterprises undertook the others. Talyllyn Railway has been in operation without a break since it was opened in 1866, its volunteer group taking over without a falter in 1951. Bala Lake Railway, built on the bed of a standard-gauge line, was started in 1972.

OVERNIGHT POINTS—Tywyn is a resort on the coastal plain of the river Dysynni. The town stretches back from the shore with the older part inland. There is an esplanade on the beach and you may stroll on the

71

sands at low tide for great distances. The village church of St Cadfan has twelfth-century aisles, nave, clerestory and north transept. Preserved at the church is the seventh-century St Cadfan's Stone which has one of the earliest Welsh inscriptions. At Talyllyn Railway Station there is an excellent railway museum. **Corris** is a slate-quarrying village in the steep valley of the Afon Dulas, just off the A487. Corris Uchaf (Upper Corris) is a mile northwest. The surrounding forest-clad slopes redeem the monotony of slate which is used everywhere—for buildings, fences and bridges. There is a small railway museum. Between the two villages, on the A487, there is a craft centre housing a number of craftsmen and their products. A mile south on the A487 is the Alternative Technology Centre, rich in energy-saving techniques. Both are worth a visit but you should check their opening times. The village church of the Holy Trinity has a fine Victorian window. **Dinas Mawddwy**, another mountain village, once a centre for slate quarrying and lead mining, is set in the upper Dyfi valley closed in by high hills. The village once had a reputation for brigandage by the red-haired Gwylliad Cochian (Red Robbers). Sharp instruments such as scythes were placed in chimneys to discourage their entry and such instruments were found in place as late as the nineteenth century. The robbers were exterminated in 1554. Merion Mills, just off the A470 at the south end of the village, is housed in old quarry buildings at what was formerly the terminus of a railway from Machynlleth. It produces Welsh flannels, tweeds and tapestries. There is a shop attached. **Llanuwchllyn** is a village near the head of Lake Bala. Its name means 'church at the head of the lake' and the church, rebuilt in 1872, contains a fourteenth-century figure of a knight. The Edwards, father and son, who did much to restore the Welsh language, lived here. **Bala** is a cheerful town with a wide, tree-lined main street, set at the foot of Bala Lake, the largest natural expanse of water in Wales. The town was once noted as a centre for the Nonconformist movement in Wales, and, in the late eighteenth century, was the focal point of a cottage industry producing woollen stockings. Every man, woman and child seemingly engaged in this activity, especially during the winter months. Visitors recorded that they saw the inhabitants sitting by the roadside or outside their cottages busy knitting. It was part of the fabric of the social life: large *cymmouth gwau* or knitting assemblies were held and more intimate *noson weu* or knitting nights when neighbours would join for the evening to knit, gossip, tell ghost stories and, of course, share food, reminiscent of the quilting bees held in rural America. The heyday of this stocking business coincided with the Methodist Revival and the *noson weu* was used as a natural place to spread the Gospel. The production figure for 1799, at the height of the boom, was 192,000 pairs of stockings covering a deal of feet including royal ones as it is recorded that George III would only wear Bala stockings for his rheumatism. We were so impressed that we each bought a hand-knitted pair, hoping they were made in Bala.

1 TYWYN-CORRIS

6½ miles (10·5km) 2080ft (630m) OS 124, 135

Talyllyn train

This is an easy introduction to the fairly strenuous two days to come. You ride in comfort on the narrow-gauge Talyllyn Railway from Tywyn to the end of the line above Abergynolwyn, walk by a forest path to an old quarry, by old tracks up valleys, finally climbing and crossing a high ridge where you will have panoramic views and will see the rest of the Walk spread out before you. You end in the slate mining village of Corris which has lost most of its inhabitants but not the evidence of the industry which sustained them. Seeing the debris from slate mining always reminds us of the conditions under which miners had to work as late as the beginning of this century. Miners worked in teams, renting access to the mine from the mine owner and selling their finished product to him; they were therefore largely at the mercy of the owners. What was unique to mining, however, was the long hours in the dark — 12 hours a day, 6 days a week, 52 weeks a year — with only a candle to light the work; most of a lifetime spent in the tiny pool of illumination cast by a candle. We always appreciate the sun and the distant views on the days we walk near mines.

Since the Talyllyn Railway may not be operating when you walk, an alternative is to start at Machynlleth, using the southern end of the Abergynolwyn–Machynlleth section of the Snowdonia Walk to Pont Llaeron (p112). This adds about 3 miles to the day.

EAST—From the British Rail station in Tywyn walk SE on the A493 for about ¼ mile to the start of the Talyllyn Railway. Take the railway to its farthest station, Nant Gwernol. From the station go up either the path on the abandoned railway bed SE of the station or cross the bridge over the Nant Gwernol to a parallel path. At a second bridge, where the two paths join, leave the paths and scramble up the NE bank to a gravel track that comes up from Abergynolwyn. Go R (SE), then R again at a fork and you will soon be walking through the lower workings of the old Bryneglwys quarry. Immediately after passing the first deep quarry hole L, go L a

73

short distance uphill to a green track running SE along the NE slope of the Nant Gwernol Valley. You pass under an old incline and reach an ancient bridge at the head of the valley (Pont Laeron, said to be an old Roman bridge). If you have started at Machynlleth, you will join this route here (p112).

From the bridge turn E on a track up a tributary valley. There is a new forest here but the track has been left undisturbed. At a low saddle, cross a stile and go L (N) along a fence up the steep, grassy, flank of Tarren y Gesail to its top (666m, 3 miles from Nant Gwernol). On a clear day the views are magnificent. To the S you see an expanse of the Dyfi estuary; to the W is Cardigan Bay with the Lleyn Peninsula NW; to the N is the full stretch of the Cader Idris range. NE you will see the ridges of your next day's journey and in the distance the top pyramid of Aran Fawddwy over which you will trudge in two days' time. E and SE are the lesser folds of the southern Cambrian Mountains.

At the ridge go R (E) along a second fence to a stile L (N). Do not miss this stile as the fence soon ends at a precipice! Beyond the stile a distinct path goes downhill to the R of an old fence that is mostly a series of posts. You descend to a saddle, a forest appearing L of the fence, and climb to a knob. As you descend you will become aware of the cliffs to the R. At the knob the fence swings L (N) and you follow it for about $\frac{1}{4}$ mile. It swings R for its final change of direction and you descend, sometimes steeply, on a grassy slope (no path), keeping the forest close to the L. Corris Uchaf will soon appear below you. Head away from the forest near the bottom of the valley to a gate and the A487. Walk E a short distance to a road L which will take you away from the busy A487 down to Corris in 1 mile. Braich Goch Hotel is to the R where the road rejoins the A487.

WEST—Walk N out of Corris on the back road to Corris Uchaf. At the A487 turn R past the village and take the first gate L on to open fields. Climb steeply S, SW and then S again along a forest edge to a knob. Follow the fence as it swings R (SW) along the spine of Tarren y Gesail, descending to a small saddle before climbing to the highest point. There will be cliffs to the L. At the highest point go S, not too steeply, into a valley. Go R over a stile to a track W that takes you to the valley running down to Abergynolwyn. At a bridge (Pont Llaeron, where you go L if ending at Machynlleth), go NW on a track along the NE slope to a gravel lane which takes you towards Abergynolwyn. As you near the village, take a signposted path L to Nant Gwernol Station. The Talyllyn Railway will carry you an easy 7 miles to Tywyn. The distances are: the knob on Tarren Gesail 2½ miles, Pont Llaeron 5 miles, Nant Gwernol Station 6½ miles.

miner's lantern

2 CORRIS-DINAS MAWDDWY
12 miles (19·25km) 1890ft (580m) OS 124

This is a long day on the sinuous ridge that runs between the two villages and is a great walk for views. You go over five small peaks, all above 600m but these rise only 100m or so above the ridge. There is some road walking at both ends but the longer stretch from Corris is on a quiet road. Your way is along the narrow valley of the Afon Dulas and then a steep-sided cwm to the ridge. You will pass the shops and mine entrance of a working slate quarry. When you gain the ridge, the mass of Cader Idris still dominates the skyline to the north but a new view is opened up of the country to the south. This is a vast stretch of hills and valleys nearly covered by the mature evergreen of the Dovey Forest. The expanse of green is laced with the dark lines of forest roads seemingly going nowhere. Looking down on it we had the feeling that you could wander lost for days if you were foolish enough to venture into the darkness of this forest.

We walked this section on a rainy, very windy day, with the mountain tops going in and out of the clouds. It was fun then and should be grand on a sunny day. The way is easy to find even in the mist, as there are fences along the ridge top as friendly guides. The footing is poor to good, but there are many boggy sections to negotiate. We rate this stretch as somewhat strenuous, especially in high winds or poor weather.

EAST—Walk E from Corris on a road along the Afon Dulas. In 2 miles, shortly after the shops of the Aberllefenni quarry, go L at a fork into Cwm yr Hengae; you will soon pass the mine entrance of the quarry on the R. The road begins to steepen and you have a stiff climb up to the end of the road. The cwm is beautifully forested and the views back make up for the climb. At a fork go R on a track to the forest edge and go R up a steep, grassy, hill, keeping a stream to the R (no path). At the top go L up to Mynydd y Waun (4 miles). A ladder stile at the fence corner identifies this point. Here you join the path up from Bwlch Llyn Bach. Head NE along the ridge, keeping the fence to your L. You dip down and climb Mynydd Ceiswyn (604m), Waun-oer (670m, with a heavy stone pillar) and Cribin Fawr (630m), all roughly on a NE heading. Cribin Fawr is a broad plateau and your route swings SE and follows either the fence or a short-cut path that comes back to the fence at a saddle. Here are two stiles. The long ridge of Mynydd Dolgoed stretches SW but do not be attracted to it. Cross both stiles and keep the fence on your R until you leave the ridge. To the L is the first of the two great cwms that face Bwlch Oerddws. The A470 passes below and you can see the cars as small moving dots. You climb SE and then E along the precipices of Craig Portas (keep well back), dip to a saddle and then climb Maesglasau (8 miles). Here the fence swings E and you do not climb to the summit. As you move down the slope of Maesglasau you will lose the path but the

76

fence gives a positive direction and you follow what looks to you like the driest ground (it won't be, of course). The second great valley, Cwm-yr-eglwys, gradually unfolds to the L. Between you and its edge is a small ravine and a stream that plunges over the precipice of the cwm in a spectacular waterfall (you will be able to see it in a few minutes). At a forest edge turn E and descend to the Bwlch Siglen. At its lowest point, a faint path crosses from a stile at the forest edge. Turn L (N) and you will find a path zigzagging down to the floor of the cwm. Take a green track along the E side of the cwm to a lane that leads in $\frac{1}{2}$ mile to the A470. Dinas Mawddwy is 1 mile to the R.

WEST—Walk W from Dinas Mawddwy on the A470 1 mile and take the first farm lane L (Tyn-y-braich). In $\frac{1}{2}$ mile go L on a signposted track and path S up the valley to the Bwlch Siglen. Go R (W) and take the long, sinuous, undulating ridge to Mynydd y Waun, following a fence. Go S to the edge of a forest and R (SW) down to a track. Go L to a road leading to Aberllefenni and then R to Corris. The distances are: Bwlch Siglen 2 miles, Mynydd y Waun 8 miles.

3 DINAS MAWDDWY–BALA
11 miles (17·75km) 2650ft (805m) OS 124, 125

Aran Fawddwy

You will enjoy the exhilaration of crossing the long ridge of the Arans. The ridge is narrow enough to give good views and long enough to provide these views for hours. You will feel you are on top of north Wales, with peak upon peak spreading in all directions. It showed us, as other mountain tops did not, just how mountainous north Wales truly is and why the Saxon and Norman invaders found the land so difficult to penetrate, just as they found the courageous, tenacious Welsh so hard to subdue.

The Arans have two principal peaks and you will traverse both. The higher, Aran Fawddwy, is the highest peak south of Snowdonia and yet is scarcely higher than the intervening ridge between the two summits. The eastern flank of the range is lined with formidable cliffs, the western with gently descending moorland.

The way is easy to find in all but misty weather, the footing good, with only a few boggy patches. The way over the peaks will seem more daunting than it will prove to be, each rocky slope having easy grass routes amongst the rocks. We suggest, if the weather is too threatening on the ridges, that you take the road through Llanmawddwy and over Wales' highest road pass, Bwlch-y-Groes, exciting in its own right (p81). This route that George Barrow and his umbrella took in 1854, which he described in his *Wild Wales*. It is 1 mile longer than the Aran route.

NORTH—From the Red Lion Inn in Dinas Mawddwy walk E on the road to Llanymawddwy. In 1 mile go L on a road signposted to Cwm Cywarch. You ascend easily through a narrow valley for 2 miles, with farms tucked in along the Afon Cywarch between steep grassy slopes. Ahead you will see the long valley of Hengwn going off to the NE. Beyond a small car park L a footpath signposted to the Arans goes R across a stream. The way is at first between thorn trees, attractive when in bloom. You are soon in the open and can see an old track, once used to

78

bring down peat, rising ahead of you along the SE slope of the cwm of Hengwn to a saddle. The gradient is easy but steady and you will be glad of a respite at the saddle (marked 568m on the map), 5 miles from Dinas Mawddwy. As you walk high above the valley floor near its head you will see far below the compass cardinal points spelt out in white quartz boulders on the green grass. At the saddle a post marks a turn in your route and you go L (NW) along a broad, slightly boggy spine running between Pumryd and Dyrysgol. Keep to the L of a fence on a path, faint at times, to Dyrysgol (731m). You will get good views of Aran Fawddwy and Craiglyn Dyfi cupped below to the E. The llyn is the headwater of the Afon Dyfi which flows past Dinas Mawddwy to its great estuary below Machynlleth. There is a cairn on Dyrysgol built in memory of an airman killed by lightning while climbing.

From Dyrysgol walk W down a small saddle (Drws Bach), go over a stile and make your way to the summit of Aran Fawddwy (907m, $6\frac{1}{2}$ miles). Although at a distance, the slope looks mostly rock, there are grassy patches that make the climb easy. The way is well marked with cairns to the summit. The views are superb. To the SW is Cader Idris, to the N is Aran Benllyn, partly obscured by the intervening grassy hump of Erw y Ddafad-ddu. A note of caution: between Aran Fawddwy and Aran Benllyn there is no visible path except in a few places and there are almost no cairns. In clear weather you will have no problem route finding but a heavy mist would make the way uncertain, slow and possibly dangerous. The E side of the Aran ridge is mostly cliffs—nerve-wracking knowledge in a mist! Our advice is to retreat if the summits seem to be in clouds for the day and take our alternative route. If caught in the mist between the two peaks and you feel unable to follow the ridge, go W off the ridge. The W slopes are all gentle grass and the A494 is less than $2\frac{1}{2}$ miles away. From Aran Fawddwy drop steeply about 100m (Aran Fawddwy possesses a menacing face but the descent is easy) and cross the broad grass and rock ridge connecting the two summits. It is about $1\frac{1}{2}$ miles to Aran Benllyn. You climb several stiles, and the land rises gradually to Aran Benllyn so that the summit comes upon you as a

Bala train

surprise. A massive low wall bars your way and, as you surmount it, you will see just ahead the summit cairn (884m, 8 miles). Now you will also see the long descending N ridge, with Llanuwchllyn and Bala Lake beyond.

The way N is slightly confusing at first. Just ahead is little Llyn Pen Aran. A fence runs past it and there are several stiles leading in different directions. The way is easiest to the W of the fence, with nothing worse than several steep but easily negotiated grass pitches. Avoid wandering E as you will soon be peering over Craig y Llyn into Llyn Lliwbran 400m below! The long ridge has three small knobs, minor peaks of the Aran range but your way is to the W (L) of all of them. A fence runs down the ridge and you keep L and then R of this fence. The route was recently negotiated with the local landowners and was therefore not well trodden when we used it. At confusing points you will find white arrows on convenient rocks. Before Garth Fawr, the last hill before Llanuwchllyn, you cross a stone wall on a stile and are confronted with two arrows pointed in slightly different directions. The correct route is W of the hill ahead, along the N–S fence. Beyond a second stile you descend to a green track (signpost here to Arans) and go R to a gravel track. Go L to the B4403 and L into Llanuwchllyn. For the Bala Lake Railway, after an underpass, go R (signposted) to the station.

Bala Lake

SOUTH—Walk SE on the B4403 in Llanuwchllyn and shortly after passing under an old railway bridge turn R on a signposted gravel track just as the B4403 goes L. In $\frac{1}{4}$ mile go R to a green track, signposted for pony-trekking, and in another $\frac{1}{4}$ mile go L at a signpost to the Arans. Make your way directly up the N ridge of the Arans along or near a fence until you reach Aran Benllyn. From here go S over the broken country of the top ridge to Aran Fawddwy. When in doubt as to route, keep to the W side of the ridge. There are few cairns and no real path. Descend from Aran Fawddwy following a well-cairned route to Drws Bach; go E over Dyrysgol and follow a track down the SE side of Hengwm to a road. Go S to a T-junction and R to Dinas Mawddwy. The distances are: Aran Benllyn 3 miles, Aran Fawddwy $4\frac{1}{2}$ miles, road in Hengwm 8 miles.

3a DINAS MAWDDWY – BALA (Lower Level Alternative)
12 miles (19·25km) 1495ft (456m) OS 125

NORTH—Continue past the turn-off for the Arans at Abercymarch and go through Llanmawddwy (4 miles) in the valley of the Afon Dyfi. At a distance of $1\frac{1}{2}$ miles beyond Llanmawddwy climb steeply through moorland to Bwlch-y-Groes (546m, 7 miles). Descend on L fork to the B4403 just E of Llanuwchllyn.

NORTH BORDERS WALK
North Wales
36 miles (58km) 4 days

Section	Distance	Overnight Points
1	8m (13km)	Y Waun (Chirk) – Llangollen
2	8m (13km)	Llangollen – Llandegla
3	8m (13km)	Llandegla – Rhuthun (Ruthin)
4	12m (19.25km)	Rhuthun (Ruthin) – Bodfari

ACCOMMODATION
(Llangollen has more than 2 hotels and guest houses listed)

Y Waun   Hand Hotel tel (0691) 772479
(Chirk)   Berwyn House (PH) tel (0691) 772698
              Plas Celyn, Pentre (GH) tel (0691) 772103
              Poplars (PH) tel (0691) 777222
Llandegla   Tegla Cottage (PH) tel (097888) 641
              Penygarth (GH) tel (097888) 696
Rhuthun   Ruthin Castle (H) tel (08242) 2664
(Ruthin)   Wynnstay Arms (H) tel (08242) 3147
              Castle Hotel tel (08242) 2479
              Colomendy (PH) tel (08242) 2748
              Cilgwyn (PH) tel (08242) 4486
Bodfari   Cartrefle Waen (F) tel (074571) 282
              Grove Goch (PH) tel (074571) 423

PUBLIC TRANSPORT
Y Waun (Chirk) train (British Rail) Shrewsbury 4 r/t dly, bus (Crosville) Wrexham, Chester freq service
Llangollen bus (Crosville) Wrexham freq service
Landegla bus (Crosville) Wrexham–Rhuthun (Ruthin) 2 r/t Mon & Sat only
Rhuthun (Ruthin) bus (Crosville) Chester 4 r/t dly Mon–Sat
Bodfari bus (Crosville) Rhyl, Wrexham 4 r/t dly Mon–Sat

This Walk takes you north from the good-sized town of Y Waun (Chirk)
to the tiny village of Bodfari. You will find yourself meeting and leaving
the long-distance Offa's Dyke Path during the four days. The difference
in scenery between the southern and northern parts of the Walk is
startling. There is sharp contrast between the level walk along the
towpath of the Llangollen Canal with its pleasant countryside so close at
hand and the up and down trek across the heather- and bracken-covered
Clywdian Hills with inhabited countryside so far away that the farms and
villages appear in miniature. Each has its own beauty. Highlights along
the way include walking over the highest aqueduct in Britain—
Pontsycyllte, Telford's masterpiece—and overnight stops at two of
Wales' most popular towns, Llangollen and Rhuthun (Ruthin). You will
climb to the ruins of an early Welsh castle perched on a steep-sided grass
cone, walk the ramparts of Iron Age hillforts and get a bird's-eye view of
the striking Horseshoe Pass.

OVERNIGHT POINTS—Y Waun (Chirk), the gateway to the
Ceiriog Valley, is a town on the Anglo-Welsh border. Its parish church
has a fifteenth-century tower and roof. Chirk Castle is nearby, its original
walls and towers of 1310 much modified by its inhabitants over the
intervening years. It is still lived in, and is open to the public. It is $1\frac{1}{4}$ miles
from Y Waun (Chirk) railway station at the end of a mile-long driveway.
Its magnificent iron entrance gates are considered to be wrought-iron
artistry at its best. The entrance is just $\frac{1}{4}$ mile off your route. **Llangollen**
has a world-wide reputation for the week-long International Eisteddfod
held there in July. The town lies astride the river Dee, its two halves
joined by a stone bridge, said to have been reconstructed in 1345. The

83

Llangollen Branch of the Shropshire Union Canal ends above the town and has a Canal Exhibition Centre. The famous Plas Newydd, with its ornamental black and white façade, once the home of the two eccentric but colourful 'Ladies of Llangollen', stands at the south end of town (open to the public). About $1\frac{3}{4}$ miles north on the Ruthin road are the extensive ruins of Valle Crucis, a Cistercian abbey founded in 1500 (partly spoiled by an adjacent caravan park) and the 1200-year-old Eliseg's Pillar, engraved with the family tree of a fourth-century prince of Powys. **Landegla** is a secluded moorland village, site of St Tecla's Well, its waters once renowned as a cure for epilepsy. The hamlet was an important point on a drove road along which Welsh cattle were driven to English markets. **Rhuthun (Ruthin)** was once a fortified town built on a hill. Its major streets fall away from a square and castle on the hilltop. Its architectural heritage is well displayed and spans seven centuries. Plas Coch, downhill on Well Street, and parts of St Peter's Church date from the thirteenth century, and Nantclwyd House just off the square on Castle Street is a townhouse of the fourteenth century. From the fifteenth and sixteenth centuries, the most dramatic examples are the half-timbered buildings, especially Exmewe Hall and the Courthouse (now housing banks) and the Myddleton Arms (now incorporated in the Castle Hotel on the square). The oak roof presented to St Peter's Church by Henry VII in recognition of the support by men of Wales at Bosworth is also from this period. The wrought-iron gates of St Peter's, the County Jail on Clwyd Street (now the library), as well as the rosy-brick Colmendy House standing beside the castle gates, represent the eighteenth century. The Ruthin Castle Hotel is a fine Victorian building set in the midst of the ruins of a medieval castle. There is an attempt to recreate the mood of its distant past in the medieval banquets held there most evenings. They are well worth attending for the music alone. When we were there we spoke afterwards with two harpists. We complimented them on their performance and spoke of our amazement that a town of this size should have two harpists. We were gently told that there were six — a reminder that the harp is still an important instrument in Wales. Indeed, the old law of bankruptcy must still be relevant — that there are two necessities the law cannot take from a household, the cooking pot and the harp.

1 Y WAUN (CHIRK)-LLANGOLLEN

8 miles (13km) negligible elevation OS 117, 126

This is an easy stroll along the towpath of the Llangollen Branch of the
Shropshire Union Canal. The only canal in north Wales, its construction
was a supreme feat of engineering because of the hilly ground. Half of the
canal is cut into rock on the slope of the Dee Valley and two tunnels, one
of which you will walk through, were needed. The centrepiece is the long
Pontcysyllte Aqueduct, exciting to cross. You will see many narrow
boats in season; there may be water rats going about their business and
almost always a duck or two. The views of the Vale of Llangollen and of
the surrounding high hills make the canal unusually scenic, as do the ferns
and wild flowers along the way. We recommend that you digress $\frac{1}{4}$ mile
off your route near Y Waun (Chirk) to see the marvellous wrought-iron
gates at the entrance to Chirk Castle, even if you cannot spare the time to
visit the castle itself. The towpath provides firm, easy walking except in
wet weather near Chirk and it is, of course, impossible to lose the way.
NORTH—From the intersection of the A5 and the B4500 in Y Waun
(Chirk) walk N on the A5 and take the first road L (W) for $\frac{1}{4}$ mile. Just
after passing over the railway, go R on a path down to the E bank of the
canal (Chirk railway station is a few yards N of the railway bridge and the
entrance gates to Chirk Castle are $\frac{1}{4}$ mile W of the canal. Once on the
towpath look back S to see the entrance of the 1380ft long Chirk Tunnel.
Walk N on the towpath through a deep wooded cutting. In about $\frac{1}{2}$ mile
you emerge from the cutting and see the fields of Chirk Castle to the L.
There is a concrete apron here on the W side of the canal, used as a
spillway for flood waters in the canal. It prevents overflow elsewhere
which might breech the earth banks. Two miles from Y Waun (Chirk)
you enter the short (560ft) Whitehurst Tunnel. The footing in the tunnel
is a bit rough and it is dark except for the gleam of the distant exit but
there is a handrail and no danger. A canal boat may hoot at the entrance to
warn other boats (it is just wide enough for one boat) or a boat may sweep

Pontcysyllte

by you, its single eye blazing in the dark. In $\frac{1}{4}$ mile beyond the tunnel the canal turns L up the Vale of Llangollen and you will catch glimpses R of the river Dee below. You will pass the ruins of six old lime kilns on the L. Watch R for a view of the impressive Newbridge railway bridge over the Dee. Ahead you will see the high hill of Dinas Bran, a landmark on tomorrow's walk. At the end of the straight stretch, you come upon Telford's magnificent Pontcysyllte Aqueduct, soaring 30m above the flood of the Dee. Built in 1805, the year of Waterloo, it is Britain's highest aqueduct. Instead of the earlier method of using a masonry channel built into a massive arched bridge, the aqueduct is a series of wrought-iron troughs bolted together, resting on slender stone piers. Nearly two centuries of life sit lightly on it. Crossing the aqueduct on the narrow footpath is a thrilling and, for some, daunting experience.

At the N end of the aqueduct is the Trevor Basin (4 miles), once a busy wharf but now a centre for pleasure cruisers. The canal takes a 90° L turn here. To reach the towpath to Llangollen cross the basin by the road bridge or footbridge and go L across the canal to the towpath on its S side. From here to Llangollen the canal runs high along the N slope of the river valley. The way is through a quiet wood where the trees meet overhead. The canal narrows as the slope steepens. When you reach Llangollen you will find yourself well above the town, looking down on the roofs of the houses. At the Canal Exhibition Centre (well worth a visit), leave the canal and walk down the road that crosses the canal here, to the A539. Dog-leg R to Castle Street and cross the bridge to the town centre.

Since the walking is so easy, you may want to continue the $1\frac{1}{2}$ miles on the towpath to the end of the canal at Llantysilio. You will pass the 'winding hole', a basin for turning canal boats, and beyond it the site of the International Eisteddfod. The canal ends at Horseshoe Falls, an impressive weir.

On your return from the end of the canal, if you still have some energy left, go L on the A542 as it leaves the canalside and walk $\frac{1}{4}$ mile N to Valle Crucis Abbey and, $\frac{1}{8}$ mile beyond, the Pillar of Eliseg (see p84).

SOUTH—From the town centre in Llangollen go N on Castle Street across Llangollen Bridge and dog-leg R to Wharf Hill Road. Just before the road crosses the canal go L to the towpath and then R (E) on the path to Y Waun (Chirk). Just before the second tunnel go L up to the road. Chirk railway station is just L and the A5 and Y Waun (Chirk) town centre are $\frac{1}{4}$ mile beyond. The distances are: Trevor Basin 4 miles, first tunnel (Whitehurst) 6 miles.

herb robert

2 LLANGOLLEN-LLANDEGLA
8 miles (13km) 1260ft (385m) OS 116, 117

This section takes you over the steep mount on which the ruins of the thirteenth-century Castell Dinas Bran perch, follows under the long face of the Eglwyseg Rocks and over a pass with views of the Rocks and the famed Horseshoe Pass to high moors leading to the quiet hamlet of Llandegla. Castell Dinas Bran, sometimes called Crow Castle, was once the home of beautiful Myfanwy, daughter of a Norman earl. She was loved by Hywel, a youthful bard of lowly birth, who tried to win her by his singing and playing. Alas, she married another and the broken-hearted young man immortalised her in a long Ode which has been a well-loved Welsh poem for over four hundred years. So she lives on while the Castell is a lifeless ruin.

Some route finding is required over the moorland, and the going will be slow there when the bracken is high; for most of the journey, however, the way is easy to follow and the footing is excellent. You are on Offa's Dyke Path for two short sections.

Llangollen

NORTH—From the town centre in Llangollen go N on Castle Street over the Llangollen Bridge. Dog-leg R to Wharf Hill Road and cross the canal. Go R up a set of steps by a signpost marked to Castell Dinas Bran. Follow the marked route uphill, past a school, across a road, up a meadow, road and path until you near the summit ruins and then take the easiest way up a long grassy slope (a favourite spot for sliding down on cardboard sheets) to the ruins of the Castell (1 mile). Cross the ruins (good views of the Vale of Llangollen) and go E downhill along a fence R to a stile and lane. Go L to a T-junction at a gate and L on a road running under the Eglwyseg Cliffs, following Offa's Dyke Path for about 1 mile. In 1 mile you will pass St Mary's Church L at a side road. Continue to the next road L, marked as Plas yn Eglwyseg on OS map, and go L a few yards to a track going R uphill along a stream in a wood. Above the wood a path leads diagonally up the steep side of the valley past a quarry spoil, through a series of gates, past two sets of ruins and through a sheep pen. The last set of ruins, marked Cae'r Hafod on the map, is in a bwlch ($4\frac{1}{2}$ miles). Look back from here to Eglwyseg Valley and the cliffs beyond. From the bwlch go NW on a grassy path on the edge of a steep valley with good views SW of the Horseshoe Pass. In about 1 mile you cross a lane leading to a radio transmitter, visible to the R. Continue NW for $\frac{3}{4}$

Dinas Bran

mile across heather and bracken to the A542. The path is faint and intermittent here but runs parallel to a stream on the R. When you reach cultivated land, follow its R edge to the road. Go R a few 100yd on the A542 to the first farm lane R and follow it $1\frac{1}{4}$ miles to Hafod Bilston, now a hiker's hostel. From the hostel take a track NW over stiles and along fences (now you are back on the signposted Offa's Dyke Path) to a footbridge. Cross and pass between cottages to the A525. Dog-leg L to a road running NW across the A5104 to Llandegla.

SOUTH—From the Hand Inn in Llandegla walk SE across the A5104 to the A525. Dog-leg L to a path between two cottages and down over a stile to a footbridge. Cross and go along a fence R to a gate with an Offa's Dyke Path signpost. Follow a path SE to a building by a forest (Hafod Bilston). Go SW away from the marked Dyke Path on a lane to the A542 and go L a few 100yd to a layby L. From here follow a faint path SE, cross a lane leading to a radio transmitter and continue SE on a clear path along the edge of a steep valley to a bwlch. Go downhill through sheep pens, and at a fork go R (S) on a path and then a track leading through a wood to Plas yn Eglwyseg (good views of the cliffs ahead on the way down). Go L a short distance to a road running S under the cliffs. Take the first lane R past Castell Dinas Bran and watch for a stile R and path up the steep side of the Castell hill. Climb to the ruins and descend W and then S on a marked path to Wharf Hill Road in Llangollen. Cross the canal to the A542 and dog-leg R to Castle Street which leads to the town centre. The distances are: Plas yn Eglwyseg $4\frac{1}{2}$ miles, Dinas Bran 7 miles.

Eglwyseg Cliffs

3 LLANDEGLA-RHUTHUN (RUTHIN)

8 miles (13km) 1370ft (420m) OS 116

This is a delightful walk that takes you from the little farming village of Landegla, through meadows, past farmhouses up on to heather-clad hills before descending to the busy town of Rhuthun (Ruthin). It is a walk of contrasts. There is the contrast between the small, seldom-visited farming hamlets and the bustling town of Rhuthun (Ruthin) with its large population of residents and visitors and with all its amenities. There is a contrast too between the desolate upland moors where only an occasional sheep grazes, and the flourishing valley pastures filled with sleek cattle and multitudes of sheep. There is even a contrast between the carefully marked Offa's Dyke Path and the unmarked way across the countryside into Rhuthun (Ruthin). The route is easy to follow and the footing is good.

Llandegla

At lunch the day we walked this route, we were joined by a young couple who were also bound in our direction. After a pleasant conversation over sandwiches, it became time to move on. There was an awkward pause. It seemed to us they would prefer to walk alone, doubtless at a faster pace, so we waited for them to leave. Finally, after much hemming and hawing, they diffidently asked if they could join us. So on we went to Rhuthun (Ruthin), a merry foursome, and we agreed to meet after dinner at a local pub. Here they confided that this had been their very first walk and that they had been worried about getting lost. When they met us they thought that with four they would at least have company if they did get lost and we did look a little more knowledge-able. They had found the day's ramble to be a marvellous experience and it boded well for their walking future. We naturally became fast friends.
NORTH—From the Hand Inn in Landegla walk NW on a gravel road, signposted with the Offa's Dyke Path marker. It becomes a path and you go along and across a stream and then through fields to the B5431. Cross

to a farm lane opposite. A short way up, look for white posts L that lead you across fields (respecting the farmer's privacy). After a stile, head for and pass R of farm buildings to a road. Go R. Where several roads and tracks cross (3 miles), keep straight ahead (N), now on a track, and go uphill along the forest edge to a television transmitter. From the transmitter climb the steep grass of Moel y Plas to the top. You will have fine views: to the E little Llyn Gweryd nestles against the forest, and W there are steep, narrow valleys with farms at their heads. Rhuthun (Ruthin) will now be in sight to the NW. You can even look back SE to Landegla, which distance has turned into a toy village. When you cross a stile you will feel a sharp contrast underfoot. The hillside changes abruptly along the fence line from grassy meadow to deep heather moor. Cross the heather to a gravel track and go R to the crest. Leave on a path L that goes round the W flanks of Moel Llanfair and Moel Gyw to a fence and stile ($5\frac{1}{2}$ miles) where there is a view of the Bwlch Y Parc and the A494 $\frac{1}{4}$ mile ahead. Here you leave Offa's Dyke Path to make your way into Rhuthun (Ruthin). Cross the stile and go L to a forest corner. Go through a gate and descend a muddy steep between two fences to a field. Go R (W) along the lower edge of the forest to a gravel track by ruined farm buildings. Take the track between the buildings to a L fork downhill through the forest, here a pleasant deciduous wood. You pass Plas-y-Nant and reach a lane at Plas-y-Nant Cottage. Continue ahead on the lane, passing a pumping station dated 1936, to the B5429. Dog-leg R to a signposted road that carries you into Rhuthun (Ruthin).

roof garden

91

Ruthin

SOUTH—From the intersection of the A494 and the A525 in Rhuthun (Ruthin) go S on the A525 a short distance and go L on Ffordd Llanrhyw Road. At the first fork go R, pass a row of houses R and go through farmland to the B5429. Dog-leg R to a lane running E, marked to Bathafarn Farm and Parc Gwyn. Go straight uphill, ignoring forks not going E. When the lane swings N, go uphill on a gravel track. After it passes between ruined farm buildings and swings S, leave it and go uphill along the S and then E edge of a forest, through a gate and across a field to Offa's Dyke Path at a stile and gate. Go R to moorland and S across the W slopes of Moel Gyw and Moel Llanfair to a track. Go R downhill a short distance and L (S) on a path and track past a television transmitter to a crossroads. Take a road S. Watch for signposts and go L across farmland, cross the B5431 to a path to Llandegla. The distances are: Offa's Dyke Path 2½ miles, TV transmitter 4 miles, B5431 5½ miles.

4 RHUTHUN (RUTHIN)–BODFARI
12 miles (19·25km) 1590ft (485m) OS 116

This is a pleasant walk over the popular northern part of the Clwydian Hills, passing through or near four large Iron Age hillforts, one with quadruple banks and ditches to foil attackers. You will visit the remains of the Jubilee Tower on Moel Fammau, the range's highest summit and, if the day is clear, will see green farmland unfolding east into England and west across the Vale of Clwyd.

What stands out in our memories of this walk is being accompanied by our six-month-old grand-daughter, Sara, carried on her mother's back. She thoroughly enjoyed it, crowing in delight when awake and sleeping peacefully the rest of the time, lulled by the rocking motion of her mother's stride. She enjoyed lunch with the rest of us in the shelter of an old stone wall. We hope the music of the gentle wind and the touch of the sun will awaken in her a love of walking on the hills. The way to and from the hills is through fertile farmland. Most of the route is signposted and easy to follow; the footing is generally good to excellent.

NORTH—From St Peter's Square in Rhuthun (Ruthin) walk E down Clwyd Street to the roundabout opposite the Craft Centre. Cross to the Mold road and, in a few yards, as it goes R, continue E on Bryn Goodman to the back of Ruthin School. Follow a footpath L behind the tennis courts. This ends at Wern Uchaf Road. Go R to a T-junction and R to two gates, side by side. Take the R gate and turn L (E) down a mud track (L gate is locked). It ends at Plas-Tower Bridge Farm. Go through the

farmyard and out along the farm lane. As it swings R and becomes better surfaced, go L on a dirt track. At the first gate in the fence on the R go through a field and through another gate uphill to a stile. Here a track, once an ancient lane, leads to the B5429. Cross and go on a road opposite (N). About 150yd beyond a school, go R on a gravel track by a farmhouse (huge oak on L). At a farm (sign 'Craven Arms, Free House') go L round a house and over a cattle grid to a field. Cross diagonally R to the upper S corner of the field, climb a gate and go S along a fence for 100yd to a gate leading to moorland. Here a muddy track goes R uphill carrying you all the way to Bwlch Pen Barras just below the car park (3 miles). Go through the car park and follow the worn track N to the summit of Moel Fammau and its Jubilee Tower. The latter was built in 1810 to commemorate the fiftieth year of the reign of George III. Originally it was a two-tiered obelisk reminiscent of an Egyptian tomb. It collapsed in 1862. What you see now is the result of a rescue preservation performed in 1970. You will find the four view indicators helpful if the visibility is good. The path continues uneventfully along the ridge. It dips to a col where a gravel track comes up from Cilcain to the E (6 miles). Continue N on the path and climb easily to the summit of Moel Llys-y-Coed (465m). You will see NW the rounded hill of Moel Arthur garlanded by the bank and ditch of an Iron Age fort. You descend steeply toward it, cross a road and climb, not quite so steeply, around Moel Arthur's NE flank on a relocation of the Path. Descend again into a saddle and dog-leg R on a lane to a small car park. Cross a stile to a forest and a junction of several forest tracks. Take a path R along the upper edge of the forest. In $\frac{1}{2}$ mile you cross the quadruple banks and ditches of a very large Iron Age fort, Penycloddiau, and go over its featureless interior to its NW ramparts (9 miles). From here your way is easily downhill, though the path is sometimes faint, to a saddle. Take a path NW that slants gently down the bracken-covered SW slope of Moel-y-Parc to meadows and by a series of signposted stiles to a road. Go L for about $\frac{1}{4}$ mile past several forks, with signposts guiding you, to a path R that crosses a meadow and stream to the A541 in Bodfari. The bus stop is to the L. B&Bs are to be found near where you came off Moel-y-Parc.

SOUTH—Walk E from the bus stop on the A541 in Bodfari about 100yd to a path R (Offa's Dyke Path sign) that leads across a footbridge and meadow to a road. Go L, following the signs. At a postbox set in the wall go R to a stile L and cross meadows for $\frac{1}{4}$ mile over several more stiles (you may have to cast about for one of the stiles but the direction is generally E slanting uphill). When you reach the moorland, a series of white posts sets you on a path slanting up the SW slope of Moel-y-Parc to a saddle. Here you touch a rough lane that comes down L from a television transmitter and goes R, not crossing the saddle. You continue uphill on short grass on an intermittent path until you cross the ramparts of Penycloddiau where the path becomes distinct. From here to the car park in Bwlch-y-Pen the path is well worn and well marked. S of Moel Arthur, just after you cross a road, there is one signpost pointing L but it does not have the acorn emblem of Offa's Dyke Path. Ignore it and go straight up Moel Llys-y-Coed on a wide swathe of sheep tracks to the path proper.

From the car park in Bwlch Pen Barras go W down the road a short distance to a green path R. Follow it downhill to fields and cross to a farm, marked Teiran. Go out of the farm lane to a road and turn L to the B5429. Cross and enter a track opposite. This ends at a stile. Cross and go downhill through a field (no path), going through two gates (ahead in the distance is Rhuthun (Ruthin) with its church spire) to a mud track. Go L to the Plas-Tower Bridge Farm and R through the farmyard to a track. At a set of gates cross to a road and go L, taking the next road L (Wern Uchaf). Go to its end to a footpath behind tennis courts to Bryn Goodman Road. Go R into Rhuthun (Ruthin). The distances are: Penycloddiau 3 miles, Moel Fammau $7\frac{1}{2}$ miles, Tieran Farm 10 miles.

herb robert

BERWYNS WALK
North Wales
31½ miles (50·75km) 3 days (circuit)

Section	Distance	Overnight Points
1	10m (16km)	Llandrillo – Llangynog
2	12m (19.5km)	Llangynog – Llanarmon Dyffryn Ceiriog
3	9½m (15.25km)	Llanarmon Dyffryn Ceiriog – Llandrillo

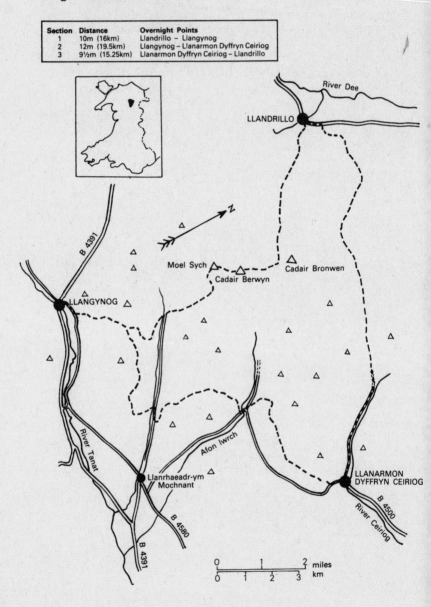

ACCOMMODATION

Llandrillo   Berwyn House (PH) tel (049084) 369
                        Boderw (GH) tel (049084) 238
                        Cadwst Mawr Farm tel (049084) 207
                        Llechan Cillan Farm tel (049084) 218
Llangynog   New Inn tel (069174) 229
                        Tanat Valley Inn tel (069174) 227
                        Cartrefle (GH) tel (069174) 258
Llanarmon   Hand Hotel tel (069176) 666
Dyffryn   West Arms Hotel tel (069176) 665
Ceiriog

PUBLIC TRANSPORT

Llandrillo bus (Crosville) Wrexham 6 r/t dly Mon–Sat
Llangynog bus (Crosville) Oswestry 1 r/t dly Mon–Sat am except Tues & Thurs, 1 r/t dly pm
Llanarmon Dyffryn Ceiriog bus (Crosville) Oswestry 3 r/t dly Mon–Sat

---

This Walk penetrates the heart of the Berwyn range. The Berwyns are
the most easterly of the great hill ranges of north Wales, and they lack the
dramatic quality of the more mountainous western ones, being mostly
gently billowing high moorland. While deceptively mild in appearance,
they can be formidable in bad weather. It was here that a Norman army
was turned back by a storm in 1164. Henry II's men—soldiers from
England, Normandy, Flanders, Gascony and Anjou—came to a sodden
halt and then retreated without ever seeing the enemy during an ill-fated
attempt to attack the Welsh near Corwen.

The main Berwyn ridge is everywhere over 600m, and the two major
peaks are over 800m. It is only here that the range is mountainous in
appearance as some 4 miles of the highest ridge are scalloped into a series
of cliffs on the east side. The centrepiece of the Walk is the high waterfall
of Pistyll Rhaeadr, claimed as one of the seven wonders of Wales. The
range is bordered on three sides by well-known river valleys: west and
north by the Dee and east by the Tanat and Ceiriog. The mountains are a
true divide as the Dee flows into the Irish Sea and the other rivers into the
Severn estuary.

The Walk is a circuit which connects small villages in these three
valleys by routes that cover the range. For two of the three days you will
be crossing the main ridge, moving over the principal summits on one of
the days. The third day you traverse the hill and valley system created by
ice and water flowing east from the heights. While the villages are small,
two of them have justly famed inns and all three are charming. Since the
Walk is a circuit, you may start and end at the same place, simplifying
your transport arrangements.

OVERNIGHT POINTS—Llandrillo is a small village in the Dee
Valley astride the Afon Ceidiog. It was once a busy droving centre but
now its major occupation is farming. The spire of the church dominates
the village, and is the first landmark noted by travellers as they approach,
whether by road or on foot. Llangynog is an equally small village at the

head of the Tanat Valley, the last village up this long trench that cuts through the Welsh hills from England. It was formerly the terminus of a branch railway from Oswestry that served slate quarries and lead mines in the valley and was once a roistering place of five inns, alive when the miners and quarrymen came to spend their pay. Today, only an occasional car disturbs the peace. The village church is dedicated to St Cynog, from whom the village derives its name. Two miles up a narrow side valley in an unspoiled setting is the remote church of Pennant Melangell, which has remarkable wood carvings. It is too far to visit on foot unless you stay an extra day but its story is too interesting not to tell. St Monacella, an Irish princess, retired here to escape a marriage. A young Welsh prince out hunting found his hounds surrounding her, held back by her presence from reaching a hare sheltering under her dress. She begged for the hare's life, and not only did the prince grant her wish but gave her a piece of land to found a religious house. The hare became her emblem. You will see it displayed on the sign of the Tanat Valley Inn in the village. **Llanarmon Dyffryn Ceiriog** is a hamlet of a few houses and two notable inns in the Ceiriog Valley. It was the home of two Welsh poets, 'Ceiriog' (John Hughes) and 'The Ceiriog Nightingale' (Huw Morris). We think it is one of the prettiest mountain villages in Wales.

1 LLANDRILLO–LLANGYNOG
10 miles (16km) 3240ft (985m) OS 125

Llandrillo

For those who love hilltops this day shows the best of the Berwyns by climbing the main ridge and going over the two principal summits. As an added fillip, you will pass one of the highest of Wales' waterfalls, Pistyll Rhaeadr, which plunges 70m from the escarpment of Craig y Mwn. We saw the falls after several days of rain and a spectacular torrent of water poured over the cliff, filling the valley below with its noise and mist. On drier days the fall of water will be much less unless it is helped as it was once for a visiting bishop for whom the stream was dammed the night

before and released, unknown to him, at his arrival. He declared the sight miraculous, to which the local minister drily answered 'amen'. There is a charming teahouse and B&B at the foot of the falls, just as you might find in the Alps.

Our route takes you between the Dee and Tanat Valleys by the long grass western slope of the Berwyns, along its highest ridge, down a narrow valley to the waterfall and then across a subsidiary ridge. The views from the main ridge are superb. The way is easy to find, the footing poor to good. For poor weather on the ridge (heavy mist, very high winds and/or low temperatures) we suggest a lower-level alternative (p101).

SOUTH—Walk E on the B4401 in Llandrillo from the bridge over the Afon Ceidiog past the health centre and war memorial to the next road R. In a few yards take a R fork to a farm (Lechwedd). The road continues as a gravel track and you climb to and along the bottom edge of a forest (good views back to Llandrillo). In about 1 mile you enter the forest briefly. As you leave the forest take a R fork to the SE. You soon have a view of the entire Cwm Pennant and the Afon Ceidiog. The gradient eases and you pass the end of another rocky track coming up from the cwm. Your track now becomes steadily fainter. Ahead you can see the next 2 miles of your journey, a grassy slope rising gently E to the main Berwyn ridge. The only landmark is a small patch of forest about halfway up. Continue E on the track along a fence to a small stream near its junction with the Afon Clochnant. The track ends and you make your least boggy way E, keeping the Clochnant at some distance on your R. You will find sheep paths and, occasionally, the old track. Beyond the small forest, which you keep on your L, the track is more distinct and you will have no trouble finding Bwlch Maen Gwynedd. Here the way is barred by a fence. Go R (S) uphill along the fence and in $\frac{1}{4}$ mile you will be on the long easy crest of the Berwyns. You will have a marvellous view in all directions if the day is clear. To the SW is the distinctive stepped ridge of the Arans with Cader Idris to the L beyond. To the W are the Rhinogs and N the

99

Clywdian Hills; E are the diminishing ridges of the border hills. You thus will see portions of three other Walks.

The fence you have followed up from the bwlch turns E and crosses the ridge to the beginning of the Craig Berwyns, the long series of cliffs and rocky steeps that comprise the E face of the Berwyns ridge for some 4 miles, with only one break. Leave the fence at its corner and walk S. The footing is best along the cliff but do not go too near the edge if the wind is high or gusty. The ridge rises and falls gently along the all-too-short $1\frac{1}{2}$ miles that you stay upon it. Cadair Berwyn (827m) is crowned with a refuge circle of stones piled up by earlier walkers. E below Cadair is a small forest, useful as a checkpoint. You can shelter in the circle out of the wind and it is a good place to eat lunch. Moel Sych (also 827m according to the map) is a disappointment, being only a cairn on a broad grass hump. A fence runs along the ridge S from Cadair Berwyn and it will lead you, in misty weather, to Moel Sych's summit cairn. The cliffs break here and your way is down the grassy SE arm that cradles Llyn Lluncaws. The cliffs above the lake are called, appropriately, Craig y Llyn. You will pick up a path on the way down, following it past the lake and down the Nant y Llyn. Near the end of the valley, cross the stream to a track on the opposite side and go down to a road and car park near the Pistyll Rhaeadr. The teahouse and public toilets are at the car park.

Go through the car park to the path to the waterfall. Enjoy the magnificent fall of water. The natural arch under which the water foams after its first long drop is probably unique in Britain. It was once partially blocked in order to provide water for the slate quarry down the valley and the groove from which a wooden flume hung can be seen running L from the arch.

Cross the footbridge below the waterfall to a path running E under Craig y Mwn. When you come to the farm beyond the old quarry, do not go through the gate but turn R uphill along a fence, making for the quarry track above. Take this stony track L, climbing by switchbacks to the top of the ridge. After the last switchback the gravel track ends. Head SW to a gate on the wide saddle between Y Clogydd and Glan-hafon. Go through and continue SW downhill to a path that turns S down Cwm Glan-hafon to a road. Go R into Llangynog.

NORTH–Follow the detailed description from section 2 (p102) to the gate on the saddle between Y Clogydd and Glan-hafon. From the gate head downhill and pick up a quarry track that takes you by switchbacks to the valley floor. When the track makes its turn L and parallels the crag and valley bottom, look straight down and pick up a fence line a little below. Leave the track and make for this fence, picking up a path that leads L under the crags to Pistyll Rhaeadr. If you miss the turn and go into the quarry, turn back to find the fence as the way down from the quarry is steep and unsafe.

Cross a footbridge under the waterfall to a car park and go N a short distance to a track L up the Nant y Llyn Valley. Cross the stream as soon as possible to a path on the opposite side. Take this to Llyn Lluncaws and climb the SE arm of Moel Sych to its summit cairn. Go N along the Berwyn main ridge to Bwlch Maen Gwynedd (first major saddle) and take an intermittent path W down the Clochnant valley, keeping well R of the stream. When you reach a fence, go W on a track along it, passing the head of a stony track to the L. You swing round N and descend through a forest to its lower edge and to a farm (Lechwedd). Take the farm lane into Llandrillo. The distances are: Pistyll Rhaeadr $3\frac{1}{4}$ miles, Moel Sych 5 miles, Bwlch Maen Gwynedd $6\frac{1}{2}$ miles and top of the forest 9 miles.

Pistyll
Rhaeadr

There is an alternative route that avoids the high ridge, although we have not walked it. Coming from Llandrillo, at Bwlch Maen Gwynedd continue SE downhill to the easier ground under the crags and go S $1\frac{1}{2}$ miles to Lluncaws. You will go over two low ridges. There appears to be a path to the first ridge and the easiest way from there seemed to us, from a view from Cadair, to pass between the cliffs and a small forest.

2 LLANGYNOG–LLANARMON DYFFRYN CEIRIOG

12 miles (19·25km) 1890ft (580m) OS 125

Llangynog

You will find this the most intricate route of all our Walks as it crosses a maze of farmland on the hills and in the valleys between the Tanat and Ceiriog rivers. There are no signposts other than the footpath signs at each end, yet you are on ancient rights-of-way for the whole day. You cross three hill ranges that run southeast from the great Berwyn ridge and dip into the valleys cut by streams running from the ridge to the river Tanat. You may misplace the way but never be lost as you are always in farmland and near roads and habitation. Yet you will hardly equate this quietly beautiful countryside with bustling civilisation. And just because the route finding will be engrossing, don't forget to take time to enjoy the passing scene.

We enjoyed Welsh singing in an unusual way while we were in Llangynog. We had retired to our inn early on a Saturday night after a long day of route finding. Our room was over the bar but the murmur of voices scarcely disturbed us as we began to fall asleep. Suddenly a piano crashed an opening chord and singing started up as if in the room with us. Initial irritation at being awoken was soon replaced by the pleasure of hearing Welsh voices in harmony and we gladly stayed awake until the impromptu concert was over.

We rate this as our most challenging route to follow. You will have every type of way—roads, mud lanes, grass tracks, paths and a few stretches without paths—in constantly changing sequence. The footing is poor to good. The OS map and our detailed directions are essential.

NORTH—Walk N on the B4391 from the New Inn in Llangynog across the Afon Eirth to the first road R. In about ½ mile go L on the farm road to Tai-glas. Pass farm buildings and caravans on the R and climb up a well-worn track which follows a stream on the L towards the head of the cwm. After fording a tributary where there are traces of an old mine, you come to a locked gate. Turn R uphill and follow the fence (no path) to another gate from which a worn grassy track slants R up to the saddle ahead. Take this track; it peters out as you near the saddle, but keep close to the rising SE flank of Y Clogydd and you will pick the track up again near a gate. You will now be able to look down into the valley of Afon· Rhaeadr. Go through the gate and turn R (E) on an old sunken track. In good visibility you can see your way ahead following a high contour on the slope of Glan-hafon. You may have some wet ground to negotiate before the track turns stony. The track ends at a sheep barn by a lane. Go L (E) and in ½ mile go L across fields down the E side of a small forest to a road. You should be just SE of a farmhouse and a ravine. Go down the R (SE) side of the ravine to a short path leading to a footbridge across the Afon Rhaeadr. Cross to a road at a small group of houses (Commins). Go R for ½ mile to a fork and L ¼ mile to a track L just beyond the entrance to a pony-trekking centre. Follow this track NW and then N, first through a

forest and then in the open, up the flanks of Moel Hen-fache. As the way levels out, you reach a gate to a cultivated field and the track ends. Do not go through the gate, but turn L (N) and follow the fence line to the next gate. Do not go through that gate either but turn so it is behind you and you will see a faint grass track ahead going N. Follow it carefully. It is discernible as a wide, slightly sunken depression and easy to lose if you don't pay attention. You will soon see Bryn-gwyn farm below and the track becomes steadily more distinct until it is stony. It leads you through the farmyard and you take the lane E to a road. Turn L past another farm lane to a fork and go L to a farm lane and telephone box at Tyn-y-ffridd. Walk N from the box past a 1907 house. In $\frac{1}{4}$ mile, just before a gate, go R through a side gate to a green track going across a small valley. Ahead, on the opposite slope, you will see a track slanting uphill to the R and this is your next section of route. Descend to the valley floor, jump a small stream, find your way through a small sheep pen and take the green track around the shoulder of Rhos. At the saddle between Rhos and Garneddwen, the track disappears beyond a gate. Go through the gate and downhill, bending to the L, to an intermittent track that goes along the NW side of a valley. When it reaches a clear track that goes S down to Pen-cae-newydd (a building in a copse), leave it and go E. Climb slightly and then descend gradually, keeping a line of thorn trees to your R. You will be N of and high above the valley on the R. Keep your line of direction to the gates. As the way steepens you will find a faint green track that will carry you down to and along a small stream to a road. Llanarmon Dyffryn Ceiriog is $\frac{1}{4}$ mile to the L.

Hand Hotel

SOUTH—From the crossroads in Llanarmon Dyffryn Ceiriog, walk S on a road $\frac{1}{4}$ mile to a path R (footpath sign). You go along a stream and then over fields SW uphill. As the gradient eases, follow a line of thorn trees SW and W. As a valley opens up L, you will see a saddle ahead between Garneddwen and Rhos. Keep to the NW side of this valley and make for a gate in the saddle. Beyond, follow a green track around the flank of Rhos to a sheep pen, cross a stream SW to a farm lane and go L to a road at Tyn-y-ffridd (telephone box). Go L and take the R fork to second farm R (Bryn-gwyn). Go up a lane through the farmyard to a track SW up Moel Hen-fache. The track becomes faint and you skirt a fence at the highest point to a gravel track going S downhill. At a road go R to a T-junction and R $\frac{1}{2}$ mile to a small group of houses (Commins). Take a lane L between houses to a footbridge; cross and go L uphill on grass to a road. Cross and continue uphill to a lane. Go R to a sheep barn and take a track R that goes round Glan-hafon to a path L that leads down to a road. Llangynog is $\frac{1}{4}$ mile to the R. The distances are: Tyn-y-ffridd 3 miles; Commins 7 miles.

3 LLANARMON DYFFRYN CEIRIOG-LLANDRILLO
9½ miles (15·25km) 1190ft (370m) OS 125

This Walk crosses the Berwyns along an old drove route to Oswestry and Shrewsbury. You will be on the section which connects the exceptionally attractive hamlet of Llanarmon Dyffryn Ceiriog (which has two old inns, a sure sign that it was a drover's stop) and Llandrillo, a quiet village today but a busy droving centre in the days before the railway. The major part of the Walk is on upland moors, but you also go through a mature evergreen forest.

The drovers and their exploits were uppermost in our thoughts when we did this walk. We regaled each other with snippets of information which we had gleaned about these Welsh cowboys from such books as F. Godwin and S. Toulson's *The Drover Roads of Wales*. As we climbed to the open moor it was not hard to imagine the sight and sounds of some hundred or so animals being driven along this way. They would have been well shod with cues (iron crescents) on their hooves. The drive

the West Arms

might have included pigs and geese, along with the little black Welsh cattle. The pigs and geese would also have had foot protection against the rigours of the long march. The geese were sent through a mixture of tar and sand or crushed shells which hardened into a protective surface, while the pigs wore woollen socks with leather soles. The drovers walked or rode Welsh ponies alongside and constantly called out as they approached farms so that the farmers would be warned to pen their animals lest they joined the drove. Short-legged corgies were the preferred herd-dogs, barking and nipping at the heels of the livestock to keep them in order. It is told that these intelligent dogs often arrived home before their masters to alert the wives to prepare for their husbands' arrival. The way is easy to follow and the footing is poor to excellent.

WEST—From the square in Llanarmon Dyffryn Ceiriog walk W on a road up the valley of the Afon Ceiriog for $2\frac{1}{2}$ miles. Go L (W) at a fork to a stony track on to the moorland, running parallel with the Nant Rhydwilym. You ascend through boggy ground to the memorial stone to 'The Wayfarer' (5 miles). The wayfarer was W. M. Robinson, an indomitable cyclist who wrote and lectured on the joys of getting off the beaten track, even to the extent of carrying one's bicycle over mountain passes. The Rough Stuff Fellowship (RSF) was organised after his death to keep alive the tradition and erected this stone in his memory. The stone could also be said to be on the main Berwyn ridge as a faint path runs S from here over steadily rising land to Cadair Bronwen $1\frac{1}{2}$ miles away.

From the 'Wayfarer' stone the track descends. In about 1 mile, at a sheepfold, you take the L fork and, further on, enter Coed y Glyn forest. The track becomes a forest track ending in a lane. Turn L, cross the Afon Llynor and go R for $\frac{1}{4}$ mile to the B4401. Llandrillo is 1 mile to the L. **EAST**—Walk N from Llandrillo on the B4401 for 1 mile and take a lane R at a telephone box. In $\frac{1}{4}$ mile take a lane L across the Afon Llynor to a forest track going uphill E through Coed y Glyn. Take a L fork to the moors and a R fork on the moors, joining another track at a sheepfold. Continue E, ascending to the highest point at a memorial stone and descending to a road running into Llanarmon Dyffryn Ceiriog. The distances are: sheepfold $3\frac{1}{4}$ miles, memorial stone $4\frac{1}{2}$ miles, and road to Llanarmon 7 miles.

a 'Rough Stuff Fellowship'?

SNOWDONIA WALK
North Wales
76½ miles (123km) 8 days

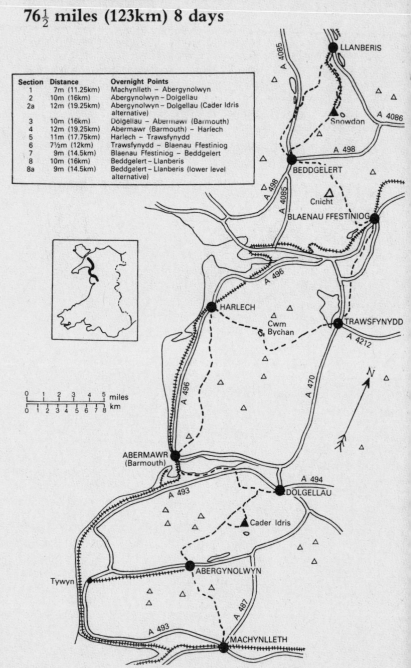

Section	Distance	Overnight Points
1	7m (11.25km)	Machynlleth – Abergynolwyn
2	10m (16km)	Abergynolwyn – Dolgellau
2a	12m (19.25km)	Abergynolwyn – Dolgellau (Cader Idris alternative)
3	10m (16km)	Dolgellau – Abermawr (Barmouth)
4	12m (19.25km)	Abermawr (Barmouth) – Harlech
5	11m (17.75km)	Harlech – Trawsfynydd
6	7½m (12km)	Trawsfynydd – Blaenau Ffestiniog
7	9m (14.5km)	Blaenau Ffestiniog – Beddgelert
8	10m (16km)	Beddgelert – Llanberis
8a	9m (14.5km)	Beddgelert – Llanberis (lower level alternative)

LLANBERIS

A 4085

A 4086

Snowdon

A 498

BEDDGELERT

A 498

A 4085

Cnicht

BLAENAU FFESTINIOG

A 496

HARLECH

Cwm Bychan

TRAWSFYNYDD

A 4212

A 496

A 470

N

```
0  1  2  3  4  5  miles
0 1 2 3 4 5 6 7 8  km
```

ABERMAWR
(Barmouth)

A 494

A 493

DOLGELLAU

Cader Idris

ABERGYNOLWYN

Tywyn

A 487

A 493

MACHYNLLETH

ACCOMMODATION
(except as noted below, overnight points have more than 2 hotels listed)

Machynlleth	Wynnstay (H) tel (0654) 2003
	Maenllwyd (GH) tel (0654) 2928
	Llys Maldwyn (PH) tel (0654) 2047
Abergynolwyn	Riverside Cafe (GH) tel (065477) 235
	R. Corney (PH) tel (065477) 278
	Tynybryn (F) tel (065477) 277
	Bodilan Fach Farm (at Llanfihangel-y-pennant) tel (065477) 231
Trawsfynydd	White Lion Inn tel (076687) 277
	Paradwys (PH) tel (076687) 392
	Preswylfa (PH) tel (076687) 279
	Fronoleu Farm (on A470 nr A4212) tel (076687) 397
	Llainwen Farm (½ mile N on A470) tel (076681) 242
Blaenau	Queens Hotel tel (076681) 203
Ffestiniog	Lyndale Hotel tel (076681) 546
	Don's Restaurant (GH) tel (076681) 403
	Lys Heli (GH) tel (076681) 799

PUBLIC TRANSPORT

Machynlleth train (British Rail) Shrewsbury freq service Mon–Sat, bus (Crosville) Wrexham freq service Mon–Sat

Abergynolwyn train (Talyllyn Railway) Tywyn 2–4 r/t dly, Apr–Oct for train or bus onward, bus (Crosville) Tywyn 2 r/t dly Mon–Sat

Dolgellau bus (Crosville) Barmouth, Machynlleth, Wrexham 5 r/t dly Mon–Sat

Abermawr (Barmouth) train (British Rail) Shrewsbury freq service Mon–Sat, bus (Crosville) Wrexham 5 r/t dly Mon/Sat

Harlech train (British Rail) Shrewsbury freq service Mon–Sat, bus (Crosville) Wrexham freq service Mon–Sat

Trawsfynydd bus (Crosville) Dolgellau 5 r/t dly Mon–Sat

Blaenau Ffestiniog train (British Rail) Llanududno Jct freq service Mon–Fri, infreq Sat–Sun, train (Ffestiniog Railway) Porthmadog freq service Mon–Sat, bus (Crosville) Porthmadog freq service Mon–Sat

Beddgelert bus (Crosville Sherpa) Porthmadog, Llanrwst 3–5 r/t dly Mon–Sat, late May–Mid Sept

Llanberis bus (Crosville Sherpa) Caernarfon freq service Mon–Sat, 4 r/t dly Sun, late May–mid Sept

---

This Walk samples the many charms of Snowdonia National Park, moving from its southern border at Machynlleth in the Dyfi Valley to the tourist centre of Llanberis on Llyn Padarn. North Wales is mountainous and this walk takes you over much high country, including two major peaks: Cader Idris and Snowdon, Wales' highest and most famous mountain. You will travel on abandoned railways, along the shore of a fjord-like estuary, through farmland, past dozens of llyns (lakes), through forests and open moors and along high ridges and mountain passes. You will stay at a variety of overnight points, from the quiet hamlet of Abergynolwyn to boisterous Abermawr (Barmouth), from mining villages to market towns, from alpine settings to seaside locations. You pass a pot-pourri of ancient monuments: an Arthurian fort, a Roman camp, standing stones and stone circles, a dolmen and the Roman Steps over a remote mountain pass. From the medieval period, Edward I's Harlech Castle and the Welsh castles of Dolbadarn and Castell y Bere guard your way.

The route is well served by public transport. For those who cannot take the time for the whole Walk, it is possible to reach and leave it at any of

the nine overnight points. Five can be reached by train and all by bus.
OVERNIGHT POINTS—Machynlleth is a market town on the
lower Dyfi Valley. A clocktower stands at the junction of its two broad
streets. There are several interesting buildings: the sixteenth-century
Parliament House, reputed to be the site of Owain Glyndwr's first
parliament in 1404, now the Owain Glyndwr Institute, and the Mayor's
House (1628). **Abergynolwyn** is a small village at the confluence of two
small rivers in the long Dysynni Valley. Its name derives from a
whirlpool which was once located at that meeting of waters. It was a
quarryman's village for the Bryneglwys quarry (now closed) and there is
a small quarry museum. Nearby is the terminus for the narrow-gauge
Talyllyn Railway that used to serve the quarry but now carries holiday-
makers and local shoppers. It is a delightful train ride to Tywyn where
there is an excellent railway museum. **Dolgellau** is in the fertile valley of
the river Wnion, where three Roman roads once met. It was a centre for
the flannel trade but is now a mecca for holiday-makers attracted to the
beauty of the area. There are several historic buildings: the Toll House on
Arran Street, recalling the days of turnpikes, and the parish church of St
Mary (1716), containing a fourteenth-century effigy of a local king.
Three hotels are of historic or architectural interest: the Golden Lion, the
Royal Queen and the Clifton. **Abermawr (Barmouth)** is a busy holiday
town at the mouth of the Mawddach estuary, caught between high dark
cliffs and the sea. Its layout is thus linear. It has a small harbour and a long
sandy beach edged by a marine promenade. King Henry VII, when he
was Earl of Richmond, lived in Ty Gwyn yn y Bermo, still standing near
the harbour. In summer there is a ferry across the estuary to the narrow-
gauge Fairborne Railway. A Panorama Walk runs along the cliffs above
the estuary, reached by a path near the railway bridge. **Harlech** is a
village of narrow streets clinging to a steep hill above a sandy plain by the
sea. It is dominated by its castle, built 1283–90, an impressive structure in a
commanding position on the hillside. The stirring song 'March of the
Men of Harlech' commemorates a doughty handful of castle defenders in
1467. The castle was last besieged in the Civil War. The town is also the
home of Coleg Harlech, an adult education centre. Theatr Ardudwy, one
of the new Welsh theatres, is in the college grounds. There is a sandy
beach, and the plain behind the beach has a rich variety of salt-marsh
plants and many uncommon birds. **Trawsfynydd** is a small village on
the large Llyn Trawsfyndd. The lake, created in 1926 for hydro-electric
power, is now dominated by a nuclear power plant on its north shore.
The attractive statue in the village square is of Ellis Evans, a Welsh
poet–farmer who posthumously won the poetry award of the National
Eisteddfod in 1917, having been killed in action just before the award, a
reminder that we are in a country where poets are still heroes. **Blaenau
Ffestiniog** is a slate mining town at the head of the Vale of Ffestiniog. It is
almost encircled by mountains whose sides are deeply marred by the

110

debris of mining. Principal attractions are the Llechwedd Slate Caverns and the Gloddfa Mountain Tourist Centre, both old slate mines where slate mining activities are recreated. They are about a mile north of the town off the A470. The town is also the terminus for the narrow-gauge Ffestiniog Railway which runs to the sea at Porthmadog. **Beddgelert**, meaning the grave of Gelert, is an alpine-like village, hemmed in as it is by mountains on all sides. Although probably named after St Kelert, it is now firmly associated with the legend of the dog Gelert, slain by his master, Llywelyn the Great, who mistakenly thought the dog had killed his child, only to find the child unhurt and a fierce wolf dead instead. The story is so good that one wishes to believe it. You can even visit Gelert's grave near the bank of the Afon Glaslyn, a 15 minute walk from the village. **Llanberis**, once a centre for the slate industry, lies on the shore of Llyn Padarn at the entrance to Llanberis Pass, surrounded by hills and mountains. Oriel Eryri, National Museum of Wales, an interpretation centre for the environment of Snowdonia, is on the bypass by Llyn Padarn. Dinorwic, one of the world's largest slate mines, stands idle to the east, under the bulk of Elider Fawr (1000m). On the opposite shore of Llyn Padarn is Padarn County Park which includes the Welsh Slate Museum within the workshops of the quarry, the Quarry Hospital Visitor Centre and the terminus of the Llanberis Lake Railway which runs steam trains the length of Llyn Padarn. Dolbadarn Castle, one of the strongholds of the princes of Gwynedd in the thirteenth century, is on the shore of Llyn Peris a mile southwest of the town. It keeps a ruined eye on the entrance to Llanberis Pass, an ancient inland route from Caernarfon to the North. There is boating, fishing and sailing on Llyn Padarn if you wish to linger here.

1 MACHYNLLETH–ABERGYNOLWYN
7 miles (11·25km) 1350ft (410m) OS 124, 135

Owain Glyndwr's parliament

This section is an old track which quarrymen from Machynlleth used to travel to reach Bryneglwys (hill of the church), a large slate quarry in the next valley to the north. You cross the river Dyfi, climb through farmland, moors and forests to a high ridge and descend through the quarry workings to the Dysynni Valley. It is a short and not strenuous walk but has enough variety of scene, footing and view to make it a satisfying journey. The way is not difficult to find; the footing is fair to excellent.

NORTHWEST — Walk N on the A487 from Machynlleth and in $\frac{3}{4}$ mile cross the river Dyfi and go L on the A493 to the first lane on the R. Climb steadily in the open, with good views behind you of the Dyfi Valley and Machynlleth. Avoid the R fork to Bron-y-aur Farm. The lane becomes a track and climbs around a shoulder to a forest. Ignore a footpath sign L here and continue ahead into the forest. Go through, crossing two forest tracks, to a newly forested area and cross NW on a level track to a second forest (3 miles). Go steeply uphill on a path through this forest, crossing one forest track, to its upper edge and continue NW along the edge to the crest of a ridge (Foel y Geifr). Go L a few yards to a stile (4$\frac{1}{2}$ miles). Below you is another newly planted slope, the ruins of the Bryneglwys quarry and, beyond, a mature forest and a glimpse of the Dysynni Valley. Go NW down through the new forest to an old stone bridge (Pont Llaeron, perhaps built by the Romans) over Nant Gwernol. The quickest route from the bridge is to continue in the same direction on a grass track along the hillside. Pass under an old incline and go L at a quarry hole to the gravel quarry track. A more interesting alternative is to descend along the Nant Gwernol. You soon come to what was once a large reservoir that

112

supplied waterpower to the quarry, its dam now breached. Skirt it and continue down by the stream. As you approach the quarry, the stream falls into a deep quarry hole in several small waterfalls. Make your way carefully round this hole and work cautiously through the quarry staying well clear of other chasms. The quarry buildings are now demolished and a new forest has been planted. Leave the ruins by the quarry track, cross Nant Gwernol and go NW down the valley for 1½ miles to Abergynolwyn.

SOUTHWEST—From the car park in Abergynolwyn walk SE up a steep lane through trees. You soon pass a path R down to the Nant Gwernol station of the Talyllyn Railway. The lane becomes a track and levels off in the open. To the R is a tree-covered slope and ahead are numerous rock piles from the Bryneglwys slate quarry. At a fork go R and wander among the rock debris of the quarry, passing a small waterfall L and a large quarry hole L (keep well clear). Go L after the hole for a short distance to a green track running along the hillside up to a stone bridge, Pont Llaeron. From the bridge go straight uphill through a newly planted forest to the ridge. An old track zigzags uphill here but is too faint to follow. At the ridge cross a stile and turn L on a path along the ridge for a few yards. By a stack of firebrooms take a path R down to and along a forest edge. The path is in good evidence from here to Machynlleth. It goes E to a corner of the forest and you plunge downhill steeply through the forest. Keep to the well-trodden L fork soon after you enter. Cross a forest track, continue downhill (a boggy stretch here), fork L and reach a newly planted area. Contour across the slope for ¼ mile, taking a R fork into another forest. The track becomes wider and goes fairly straight and mostly level, crossing two more forest tracks. You come into the open by a footpath sign R (which you ignore) and continue ahead round a shoulder. The Dyfi Valley and Machynlleth come into view. Go steeply down a steadily improving track and then lane to the A493 and go L for ¼ mile to the A487. Machynlleth is ¾ mile R, across the river Dyfi.

113

2 ABERGYNOLWYN–DOLGELLAU

10 miles (16km) 1800ft (550m) OS 124

This is a relatively easy way over the Cader Idris range by a pony path that goes over the one feasible point in the long, cliff-lined west ridge. Your route goes through the Dysynni and Cader river Valleys past Castell y Bere and the hamlet of Llanfihangel-y-pennant, over the grass and rock ridge to Llyn Gwernan and through steep foothills to Dolgellau.

Castell y Bere is one of the few strictly Welsh-built medieval castles. It was raised by Llywelyn the Great in about 1221 and it stands on a rocky spine rising out of the flat valley floor, a naturally defensible location. Like so many ruins the remains are scanty and your imagination is needed to raise the walls to their original height and to people the battlements with fierce Welsh warriors.

Near Llanfihangel-y-pennant is the birthplace of Mary Jones. In 1800, as a young girl, she walked 25 miles to Bala to buy a bible from the Reverend Thomas Charles, saving her shoes by going barefoot much of the way. His stock had run out but he was so moved he gave her one of his own. From that incident grew the British and Foreign Bible Society.

You will pass near Craig yr Aderyn (Bird Rock) (240m), a nesting area for cormorants. It is 3 miles from the sea and, since cormorants normally nest by the water, it is mute evidence of the flooding of the valley in ancient times and of the ancestral memory of the cormorants. The way is easy to follow, the route is well trodden and the footing is good to excellent.

NORTH—From the car park in Abergynolwyn walk NW on Llanegry Street and cross Afon Dysynni to a narrow road running near the Dysynni. In about 1 mile you pass Cae'rberllan on the R, built in 1590, possibly on the site of a Roman fort. Continue to a crossroads and go R, now in the valley of the Afon Cader. Ahead you will see the Castell y Bere, behind is Bird Rock. At 2 miles you pass the Castell to the L, and in another $\frac{1}{4}$ mile you will go through the tiny village of Llanfihangel-y-pennant. The parish church on the L has a leper window. About $\frac{1}{4}$ mile

Bird Rock from Castell y Bere

Cader Idris

beyond you cross the Afon Cader. R of the bridge is the ruined cottage of Mary Jones and a monument. Beyond the bridge go R along the Cader on a lane lined with beeches. At the buildings of Gwastadfryn, the lane becomes a stony track. After passing through a double gate, take a grassy track to the R (white painted post here and at strategic points ahead). You cross a tributary stream of the Cader on an old stone bridge and climb up the track, often in a deep grassy trench worn by the hooves of ponies. When you come to a wall, go L along it, looking back for the last time at Castell y Bere. Ahead Pen y Gadair, the summit of Cader Idris, will soon be seen on the horizon. You will rejoin the stony track beyond a standing stone. Go R, keeping L at a fork, and continue past the ruins of Hafotty Gwastadfryn, forking R to a stile. Go R (E) and follow a path uphill to another stile. You will be back on the grassy pony path and will climb, steeply at first, then contour E and climb gently to Rhiw Gwredydd (6 miles), marked by intersecting fences, 2 stiles and a sign '1842', giving the height of the spot in feet. N are the low foothills of Cader Idris and the Mawddach estuary. The path to the summit goes R here. You continue N on the pony path and descend to a road by Ty Nant Farm. Go R on the road to the NE end of Llyn Gwernan. Leave the road and go N (L) across the flat grassland by the lake to a path under the rocky hill beyond the lake (8 miles). Go R (NE) on the path round the hill to a road at Gelli-lwyd (house and ruined buildings here). Go R on a road downhill to the A493 on the outskirts of Dolgellau. The town centre is to the R.

SOUTH — Walk W on the A493 from Dolgellau. On the outskirts of the town take the signposted Cader Idris road L uphill. In 1 mile take a R fork to the buildings of Gelli-lwyd. Here a path goes L by a ruined barn to Llyn Gwernan. Leave the path and cross the foot of the lake back to the Cader Idris road. Go R and, after passing a car park R, take the pony path L at a telephone box. You climb S to the only break in the precipices, Rhiw Gwredydd, and go downhill on an indistinct grassy path, going over a stile en route. There are good views ahead of the Cader Valley. After the next stile, turn W (R); the path becomes a grass track and you

115

descend to a stile by a gravel track. Go L down this track, passing another track on the R. After the ruins of Hafotty Gwastadfryn, watch for a marker post and path L with a standing stone by the path a short distance away. Take the path and pass along a stone wall. Castell y Bere and Bird Rock come into view ahead. Follow the wall, passing a gate L that dramatically frames Mynydd Pencoed, turn R and zigzag downhill steeply (path slippery when wet) to a stone footbridge. The path ends at a stony track and you go L past buildings to a lane that runs down Cader Valley, past Llanfihangel-y-pennant and Castell y Bere to a crossroads. Go L to Abergynolwyn. The distances are: Llyn Gwernan 2 miles, Rhiw Gwredydd 4 miles, Llanfihangel-y-pennant 8 miles.

2a ABERGYNOLWYN–DOLGELLAU (Cader Idris Alternative)
12 miles (19·25km) 2900ft (880m) OS 124

You can climb to the summit of Cader Idris (The Chair of Idris) from the Pony Path and descend from the summit either by the Fox's Path or by retracing your steps to the Pony Path. The former is rated as dangerous but takes you into the magnificent cwm of Llyn y Gadair. Retracing your steps to the Pony Path adds another mile to your journey.

NORTHEAST—At the two stiles in Rhiw Gwredydd (see section 2, (p115), cross the first stile to a well-trodden path R along the L side of a fence. Climb steeply, following the cairns faithfully (not just to keep to the route but to minimise erosion). There are alternate steep and level stretches until you see Pen y Gadair ahead. The gradient eases and you veer L to the cliff edge overlooking Llyn y Gadair. The llyn is the seat of the Chair of Idris, the cliffs encircling it the arms. The notch L is known as Idris' Table. Go R along the cliff, staying well back from the edge. The route is poorly marked with cairns here until you begin to climb a steep stretch among large rocks. You will catch a glimpse of Llyn y Gafr below. In a short distance you reach the summit cairn, $7\frac{1}{2}$ miles from Abergynolwyn. Just W below the summit is a mountain refuge hut. For the Fox's Path, go from the summit a little way along the E ridge to a path going NW steeply down a scree slope (take great care here) to the shore of Llyn y Gadair. Swing NE and descend not quite so steeply to Llyn y Gafr and then NW to Ty Nant Farm (9 miles). From here follow the directions of section 2 (p115). (Note: if you forego the Fox's Path, as you retrace your way from the summit, be sure to keep to path R (W) as the path L is the Minfford Path.)

116

3 DOLGELLAU–
ABERMAWR (BARMOUTH)

10 miles (16km) 800ft (240m) OS 124

Dolgellau

This section combines a hill walk and a waterside amble in one day, wandering among the foothills of Cader Idris and strolling along the shore of the lovely Mawddach estuary, crossing its mouth on a long foot and railway bridge to Abermawr (Barmouth). The estuary, some 5 miles long and a mile at the widest, is bordered by high hills, making it look like a fjord when covered by the tide with a blanket of blue water. At low tide its appearance is changed dramatically since most of it dries out, leaving white sand gleaming in the sun. The view from the shore is charming but from the bridge at high tide it is arresting, as you can so clearly see the steep hillsides pressing in on the water. The way is mostly easy to follow; it is not strenuous and the footing is good to excellent.

WEST—From Dolgellau follow section 2 SW to Gelli-lwyd (p115). Take the track L to beyond a ruined building and head R (W) uphill on open land to the L of a stone wall. In about $\frac{1}{2}$ mile you reach a gate in a second wall stretching across your route (you may have to cast about a little to find this gate). From the gate a path between walls carries you to a barn and a farm track that goes steeply down past Hafod-dywyll to a road by the King's Youth Hostel. Go N on this road down to the A493 (4 miles) and dog-leg L to road signposted 'Abergwynant Farm'. Leave the road when it turns L over a bridge and continue ahead on a track along a stream. Beyond a gate with a sign 'private forest', go L on a path beside the stream through a beautiful wooded area with many rhododendrons. In a short distance you round a bend to a view of the estuary and a railway embankment standing as a barrier between you and the estuary. Cross a

117

small wooden footbridge and scramble up the embankment. If you are unlucky with the tide, you may have to wade a bit here. We were, and with boots off we crossed the shallow but cold water. Go L on the footpath along the top of the railway embankment. You will have mostly thickly wooded slopes close to the L and the open water of the estuary always R for the next 3 miles. You will pass a small peninsula jutting into the estuary, a perfect picnic spot with tables and benches provided. You will notice small buildings at intervals close by the railway bed and can conjecture their original and current uses. The embankment remains well above the water and has steep stone banks in places on the water side.

Where the railway bed leaves the shore of the estuary, cross a stile to a road and go R to a footpath sign and path to the L. Take the path across flat country, following footpath signs for $\frac{1}{2}$ mile, to a short embankment by the estuary with a road on top. Go L (W) on the road, pass behind a group of houses and take a track W along the estuary round a promontory. You will come to a causeway leading across a tidal flat to a railway embankment. At low tide this can be safely crossed with shoes on. At other times you can continue along the edge of the flat to a higher causeway leading to the railway. Go R on a footpath on the railway embankment and cross the estuary on a railway and footbridge to the A496 in Abermawr (Barmouth). The town centre is to the L.

Abermawr

EAST—Walk E from Abermawr (Barmouth) town centre to the railway and footbridge over the estuary and cross to the S shore. At the end of the bridge take the first or second causeway L across the tidal flat (depending on the tide) and follow the shore line E on a track, passing behind a group of houses to a road E. Pass one footpath sign, cross a short embankment and go R at the end of the embankment by another footpath sign. For the next $\frac{1}{2}$ mile follow footpath signs across flat land to a road. Go R to an abandoned railway and go L on it along the estuary for 3 miles. At the second bridge on the railway bed, go R on a path along the E bank of a stream (bridge is recognised by the stream having paths on both sides, leading off the railway embankment). Follow the path to a track R that leads in a short distance to the A493. Dog-leg L to a road going uphill to the King's Youth Hostel. Take a track L between the hostel buildings. In a few yards there are two signs: R to Cader Idris, straight on to Hafod-dywyll. Continue ahead through a farmyard and up a steep hill to a stone farm building. Pass R of the building to a track E between stone walls. Take this path to a gate and cross open moors E down to a road at Gelli-lwyd. Go R down to Dolgellau. The distances are: beginning of estuary walk 1½ miles, end of estuary 5½ miles, youth hostel 7 miles, Gelli-lwyd 8¼ miles.

4 ABERMAWR (BARMOUTH)–HARLECH
12 miles (19·25km) 1700ft (520m) OS 124
SNP Harlech, SNP Cader Idris–Dovey Forest

This section is a pot-pourri of moorland, low mountain passes, meadowland, farmland and woods along the western slope of the Rhinog range. You will have distant views of mountains, moors and the sea, and near views of grazing animals and crops, Abermawr (Barmouth) and Harlech Castle. You will have an ancient dolmen to study, a lake to rest by and, if he is at home, a maker of walking sticks to visit. The dolmen is the remains of a burial chamber, a large stone slab on top of smaller ones. It is called Arthur's Quoit and is said to have been thrown by that busy king from the nearby hill of Moelfre, the marks on it being the impressions of his fingers. The northern half of the route is a fairly complicated one across farmland, and we recommend the SNP Harlech map, one of the 1:25,000 series for Snowdonia National Park, rather than the normally adequate 1:50,000 series. The footing is fair to excellent.
NORTH—Opposite the railway station in Abermawr take the street going E up to St John's Church. At the footpath sign L of the church take a path uphill. Beyond some houses, turn R to a grassy track slanting easily uphill. You will pass several mine tunnels L and, beyond a gate, a clear grassy area and bench. At a fork go R. The track, now marked by yellow

painted arrows, zigzags up to a second fork. Go L (arrow beyond), and pass some ruins and houses. The track becomes faint, but you continue in the same direction to the edge of a valley. Go R on a narrow grassy track (two black arrows beyond) and through an opening in a wall (sign 'to Barmouth' pointing back). Go L through a gate and head across a small valley to a farmhouse (Cellfawr) $\frac{1}{4}$ mile away. Go through a gate to a path along a fence R (several arrows here) and pass in front of ruined barns. Ignore yellow arrows beyond and go L up a grassy track behind the barns. The track curves R and climbs round a hill. At a fork go L round and above a barn. Follow the track up into Bwlch-y-Llan ($1\frac{1}{2}$ miles from Abermawr (Barmouth). Go through a gate to a fork R and on through the bwlch. Follow the path slanting L downhill (several gates along the way). Above a roofless barn near Sylfaen Farm, you go through a stone wall and head up round a shoulder of a hill to Bwlch-y-Rhiwgyr. The path becomes more distinct and ascends at an easy slant N. Go through the bwlch (3 miles) and descend NW on a well-defined path that becomes a track (once a drover's road). Follow it for 2 miles to a lane. Go L, cross the Afon Ysgathin and continue N. You pass Coytan Arthur (Arthur's Quoit) on the L and come to a gate. Go R to another gate (E) and in a few yards go L through a gate and N and then E along a high stone wall to a second wall N. Walk along the wall and then continue N by a ditch and the remains of a wall across poor grassland for 1 mile (no path) to farm buildings, and take a track N past a farmhouse to a road. Go R for a short distance to a junction (sign W to Dyffryn Ardudwy and E to Cwm Nantcol). Go L (N) for $\frac{1}{4}$ mile to the first road R. You pass through farmland and, in 1 mile, descend through a pretty deciduous wood to a small valley. Some way down, a track goes R a short distance to a lake, a quiet spot for a picnic, rest or swim. At the bottom of the valley, between two bridges, you pass a group of houses (walking-stick maker in last house). Cross the second bridge and go W for $\frac{1}{8}$ mile to a road sharp R opposite an unnamed church (9 miles). Go uphill to first fork R and on to a farm (Hafod-coed). Pass R of the farmhouse to a gravel track that ends at a lane before Gwarn Einion Farm. Go R and pass through its farmyard (sign to Harlech here). Continue N for 1 mile, the lane becoming a rough track, to a farmhouse (Tyddyn-du) and go E along the farm track to a road. Go L $1\frac{1}{2}$ miles to Harlech.

SOUTH—Walk S on the B4573 from the Information Centre in Harlech and take the second road L (Fford-Uchaf) uphill. Past the youth hostel, go L on a green track between old walls (yellow arrow here) and come out on walled fields above the sea. The track goes to the L of some new houses. Under a powerline go L 100yd to a stile over a stone wall and follow the wall uphill to an opening and a track between walls to a road. Go L for $\frac{3}{4}$ mile to a crossroads and go R $\frac{1}{2}$ mile to the first farm track R (Tyddyn-du). Turn S at the farm on a rough track that will carry you in 1 mile to the farm of Gwarn Einion. Take the farm lane S, and just beyond the farm gate go L on a gravel track downhill to a road by another farmhouse. Continue S downhill, joining another road coming in R and reach a valley at a third road by an unnamed church. Go sharp L to an intersection, R over a bridge and R again over a second bridge. Go S steeply uphill on a road in a deciduous wood and through farmland to a T-junction. Go L for $\frac{1}{4}$ mile to a second junction and dog-leg R to the first gravel track L. Go down past a farmhouse and L round a barn. From here go S across grassland to pass well L of the trees on the skyline. Go along a ditch and ruined wall and then by a high stone wall to its end. Go L round a walled field to a dirt track. Go R for a few yards to a road (to Corsygedol) and immediately go L (S) on a road to a bridge. Cross and go E a short distance to a gate on the R. Ignore the yellow arrows ahead and go through gate to a path SE to Bwlch y Rhiwgyr. Beyond the bwlch the path swings S and slants down across the hillside and then climbs up to a track through Bwlch y Llan. Beyond the bwlch take a L fork that goes S. Near a barn take the R fork to pass behind several ruined buildings. Turn R in front of them on a path with fence L to a gate and gap in the wall (sign to Barmouth here). Go down the grassy track and L across an open field to reach another track descending between ruined buildings to a junction of three tracks, all with yellow arrows. Go R downhill and follow yellow arrows in reverse down to Abermawr (Barmouth). The distances are: two bridges 3 miles, Corsygedol 6$\frac{1}{2}$ miles, Bwlch y Rhiwgyr 9 miles.

Harlech

5 HARLECH–TRAWSFYNYDD
11 miles (17·75km) 1825ft (560m) OS 115, SNP Harlech

This is a walk over the Rhinog range, crossing the broken country of the
western foothills to remote Cwm Bychan, climbing the famous Roman
Steps over the Rhinogs to a forest and the bleak moors that lead to Llyn
Trawsfynydd and the village of Trawsfynydd. Around Cwm Bychan
you may be lucky enough to see feral goats from one of the two wild goat
herds in Britain. They are shy and you will see them only at a distance but
they are distinctive in their parti-coloured coats of black, brown and
grey.

Roman Steps

The centrepiece to the Walk is the Roman Steps, a stretch of narrow
paving stones in shallow steps that leads from above Cwm Bychan
through the pass between Rhinog and a lesser peak. They are part of a
packhorse path built in medieval times but later attributed to the Romans.
Their fame has spread far and wide and they attract many visitors, most of
whom come by car to Cwm Bychan. This fame creates unreasonable
expectations and we met several disgruntled people on the Steps who felt
their effort wasted. We found we became vehement advocates of this
visually modest artefact. It was clearly such an important link in the lines
of communication between the coast and the interior that some medieval
prince felt impelled to have it paved, much as you find it today. Imagine
the generations of pack-animal trains plodding up and down the Steps. It
is amazing that they have lasted nearly intact after the long centuries of
wear and weather. Their medieval users must have been startled to find
this paved way in a Wales that had so few roads. How easy to assume that
the builders were Roman since the only other roads were known to have
been built by the legions. The way is mostly easy to follow with only one
or two stretches that are at all challenging, and the footing is generally
good.
EAST—From the castle in Harlech walk E across the B4573 and go
uphill on a road. At 1 mile go L at a crossroads. In 1½ miles take a track

going R, marked 'no vehicular access, no parking'. In a few yards it forks and you go R on a grassy track. Head generally E round the base of Moel Goedog, crossing green fields and going through a number of gates. You will have ample views S and W. In about 1 mile you pass between two small crags and begin to descend. You will see Cwm Bychan ahead. Soon the track turns N and you leave it and go E downhill through gates in two walls, angle R and go through the gate on the L. Turn R downhill and go R at the next gate to a path on the top of a buried watermain. Follow the path which soon diverges from the main E downhill to where two walls meet in a 'T'. Go S and then E for $\frac{1}{8}$ mile to a farmhouse (Cwm-mawr). Pass S of the farmhouse and go SE across the head of a valley (no track) to a track going E over a saddle. Descend from the saddle to a road going along the edge of Llyn Cwm Bychan. Go E to a car park and sign to the Roman Steps (5 miles). Go through the car park to a path S that climbs easily through a sparse deciduous wood. In about $\frac{1}{2}$ mile the first slabs of the medieval Roman Steps appear. Evidence of the old packhorse route grows steadily stronger until you are on a long flight of shallow steps leading through Bwlch Tyddiad (6 miles). At the top of the bwlch you have a view ahead of the Coed y Brenin forest and hills beyond. Go downhill on a well-worn path following a stream. Do not descend all the way to the forest edge ahead but, at about $\frac{1}{4}$ mile above the forest, contour L through heather to a corner of the forest. Follow the edge NE to where two forest rides (open swathes) enter the forest. Take the L ride NE to a gravel forest track (7 miles). Go L for $\frac{3}{4}$ mile, keeping watch for a path crossing the track (yellow arrows) soon after the track swings E. Go L on a path along a stone wall, R through the wall (yellow arrows) past a roofless house (Hafod-Gwynfal) to the forest edge. Go N across moorland, following a series of widely spaced yellow painted posts. You move along a flat ridge and down a long slope leading NE to the Afon Crawcwellt at a farmhouse (Wern-fach) (9 miles). Pass L round the farmhouse to a bridge and take a dirt farm track NE to a road. Go R for $1\frac{1}{2}$ miles to Llyn Trawsfynydd. Where the road runs under an embankment along the lake, climb to the embankment top and go R to the $\frac{1}{4}$ mile long footbridge across the SE end of the lake. Cross to Trawsfynydd.

Trawsfynydd

WEST—From Trawsfynydd town centre take a road W through the town for $\frac{1}{4}$ mile to a footbridge over the lake. Cross to a road and go R (W) to the first fork L. Continue to a sign noting end of public footpath and go L (SW) on a farm track to a farmhouse and bridge. Pass R of the house and follow yellow painted fence posts and then single posts up a long slope on moorland to a flat ridge (cairn seen here for some distance). Follow the ridge to the forest edge. Yellow arrows lead you through the forest to a gravel track. Go R on the track for $\frac{3}{4}$ mile and take a forest ride going R to forest edge (if you miss this ride you can take another one just before a small concrete bridge, going sharp R). Go L (SW) along the edge of the forest until you can look down to the bottom of a narrow valley and a stream running into the forest. Contour R (W) across heather to meet the stream higher up. You will encounter a broad path by the stream. Climb moderately steeply to the top of Bwlch Tyddiad and descend on the Roman Steps to Cwm Bychan. When you reach a car park and road, go L on the road. At the last stone wall, about mid-way along the lake, take a path R uphill beside the wall for 100yd. At a fork go L (W) on a path that ascends easily to a saddle and go down into a small valley. Go across the head of the valley (no path) to a farmhouse (Cwm-mawr). From the farmhouse your way is W uphill by the best sheep path, finding the gates in the stone walls across your route. Near the highest point you will pick up a worn grassy track that comes in from the N and swings W. This will carry you between two crags and across green fields to a road. Go L downhill for $1\frac{1}{2}$ miles to a crossroads and go R to Harlech. The distances are: Coed y Brenin forest edge 3 miles, Roman Steps 5 miles, Cwm Bychan 6 miles, Cwm-mawr 7 miles, road $8\frac{1}{2}$ miles.

6 TRAWSFYNYDD–
BLAENAU FFESTINIOG
7½ miles (12km) 500ft (152m) OS 115, 124

Tomen y mur

You can look on this section as a rest day in the long walk from Machynlleth to Llanberis as it is short and the elevation gained is small. You can therefore walk more leisurely, and pay more attention to the countryside and the items of interest along the way. These include a Roman fort in which was later built a Welsh motte, a tiny Roman amphitheatre, a small torrent billed as a waterfall and the village of Ffestiniog, not to be confused with its big slate sister of the north. Your way will be mostly over farmland; the route is reasonably easy to follow, the footing poor to good.

We recommend that, as this is such an easy day, you visit one of the old slate workings north of Blaenau Ffestiniog that have been converted into centres for visitors, either the quarry of Gloddfa Mountain Tourist Centre or the Llechwedd Slate Caverns.

NORTH—Walk N from Trawsfynydd village square to the A470 and cross to a path between stone walls (footpath sign). In a few yards go L along a wall to a farm building and head N to a line of trees where you pick up a track going downhill. You will be mostly on this track until you reach the Roman amphitheatre. It will be muddy or dusty in places, depending on the weather. When you reach a road, dog-leg L to a track and a stone bridge (Pont Islyn). An abandoned railway will be to the R above you. Take the track for a short distance beyond the bridge. At a farm lane marked to Llwyn-crwn go R, cross the railway on a bridge and immediately go L on a track. Soon the sharp mound and low walls of Castell Tomen y Mur will appear. Beyond a stream the track disappears and you go N along a stone wall and then fence to the amphitheatre and a gravel track (2 miles).

If you visit the fort you will find the usual Roman quadrangle. Built in 78 AD and covering some 5 acres, it was abandoned 50 years later. It was meant to be permanent as it had stone walls, which still stand head-high in places. After the Romans, the local chiefs of Ardudwy built a castle mound inside the Roman walls. The amphitheatre is so small that it was probably used for sword instruction and other martial arts rather than the spectacles we usually associate with amphitheatres.

From the amphitheatre go R on the gravel track and follow it for about 1 mile, first through moorland and then forest, down to the A470. Go L for $\frac{1}{4}$ mile to a footpath sign and stile on the R. Cross and take a faint green track N downhill. You go under the Mineral Railway which serves the Trawsfynydd nuclear power station and go R of a farm (way is well marked) to its access lane. Go out to a road and dog-leg R, cross a stile and descend across fields into the little valley of the Afon Cynfal. Here the river runs in a series of cataracts; paths along the stream afford a better view of the Cynfal Falls and are worth a digression. Cross the afon on a footbridge and take a track NW along the side of a hill to a farm building; cross a stile and small stream just under Ffestiniog. The least muddy way from here is to cross the field W on a contour to a gap in a hedgerow and go R uphill to the B439 in Ffestiniog (4 miles). Go R to the A470 and walk NE towards Blaenau Ffestiniog for $\frac{1}{2}$ mile. L Opposite a layby, take a lane. for $\frac{1}{4}$ mile, and at a house marked 'Pandy' go L downhill. The house was once an old mill and there are millstones and other smooth rocks in the grass below it, a good place for lunch. Go downhill on a path along a tumbling stream with many small waterfalls to a signposted path R (NW) that crosses grassland. Cross two roads and at the third (B4414) go R several 100yd to the entrance of a sewerage plant to the R. Go up its access road to a path that skirts its L side. Beyond the plant you have to negotiate a series of stepping stones across a marsh to an old track that climbs N up the Cwm Bowydd. At its head you reach a town street of Blaenau Ffestiniog. For the town centre go N to the A470 and then R.

SOUTH—Walk W on the A470 from the car park in Blaenau Ffestiniog and take the street L one turning before the B4414. Go to its end and take a track going down Cwm Bowydd to the B4414. Go L and just beyond the first bend take a signposted path L. Cross two roads, and at a stream in a deciduous wood go L uphill to a road, R to the A470 and R again into Ffestiniog. Take the B4391 a short distance W and at the second footpath

the Moelwyn

sign L go downhill beside a hedge to its first gap and L across a field to a signposted path that carries you past Rhaeadr Cynfal to the A470. Cross to a footpath sign opposite, and go S across moorland to a gravel track (intermittent path). You may reach the track at any of a number of points. Where ever you do, turn on the track to reach the E edge of a line of evergreen trees at the Roman amphitheatre. Go S from the amphitheatre along a fence and wall to a stream and track beyond. Take this track to a lane and go R over a railway bridge. When near the A470, go S on a track to a stone bridge and lane. Dog-leg L to a track S uphill and follow it to Trawsfynydd. The distances are: Ffestiniog $3\frac{1}{4}$ miles, Roman amphitheatre $5\frac{1}{2}$ miles.

7 BLAENAU FFESTINIOG–BEDDGELERT
**9 miles (14·5km) 1870ft (570m) OS 115,
SNP Snowdon & Harlech**

This section takes you into country over 600m, liberally sprinkled with many high lakes and a number of mountain peaks, of which Moelwyn Mawr is the highest and Cnicht the most striking. The area around and near Blaenau Ffestiniog has been extensively quarried in the past and the route takes you through two large quarries now deserted, with their buildings in ruins. Between the quarries you pass a lake lying in a classic cwm. From the upper quarry the way is over high moors broken by ridges and small valleys until you go over the long NE ridge of Cnicht, drop down past two more lakes and descend through broken country to Llyn Dinas, from which it is an easy stroll into Beddgelert. You will pass near a legendary hillfort, Dinas Emrys, above the shore of Llyn Dinas. The fort is connected to the Arthurian legends through Vortigern, the Celtic chieftain who is blamed for first inviting the Saxons into Britain, and Ambrosius Aurelianus (Emrys is Welsh for Ambrose), who was *Dux Bellorum* (war leader) of the Britons before Pendragon and Arthur. The legend is that during construction of the fort the walls fell down each night. Vortigern was told to sacrifice a fatherless boy to prevent further destruction. For this he chose young Ambrosius. Ambrosius, however, avoided this fate by telling of red and white (Celtic and Saxon) dragons fighting underground beneath the walls and by showing how to release them. Thus the fort was built and Ambrosius lived to continue the legend. Other versions of the legend have Merlin instead of Ambrosius in the hero's role. Archaeology only shows that the fort was occupied in Arthurian times by someone fairly prosperous and therefore probably an important prince. The way is not difficult to follow, the footing is good except for a short boggy section.

from Blaenau Ffestiniog

WEST—Walk W on the A470 from the railway station in Blaenau Ffestiniog and go L on the A496. When the A496 goes L downhill continue ahead past a school and a bus depot to a road going L. In 200yd a footpath sign points R to a path leading to a footbridge over the railway. Cross and walk L up a grass and rocky slope until you pick up a path, marked with yellow painted arrows, leading SW under cliffs to a road 1 mile from the railway station. Go R uphill. By a waterfall the road becomes a gravel track going steeply uphill with a vast slope of quarry debris on the R. In ½ mile you reach the S end of Llyn Cwmorthin in the glacial hanging valley of Cwmorthin. Cross the exit stream of the lake to a track along the SW side of the lake to the head of the cwm and go up the Bwlch Cwmorthin to a flat col filled with the remains of quarry buildings. Take a well-marked path N and climb moderately steeply past Llyn Cwm-corsiog. Swing NW on a path well marked with cairns across a series of small ridges to a low saddle (4 miles). Ahead is a broad, shallow, grassy valley with a large lake, Llyn yr Adar, distinguished by a bright green island. Behind is Moel-yr-hydd and S is Llyn Cwm-y-foel beyond the dam of which there seems to be only empty air. Walk down along the E and N banks of Llyn yr Adar to a path going N over a small notch, and go steeply down into a valley containing Llyn Llagi. Pass R and well above the lake and over boggy ground to a road by houses (6 miles). Cross the road, pass L of a white house and climb a low hill E. From here you will see a small evergreen plantation and another white house beyond. Your way is by a faint path that goes by the plantation and L round the house. Behind the house there is a fairly well-defined path going downhill through rhododendrons, over rolling moors and a deciduous forest to Llyn Dinas (7 miles). Go L along the shore of the lake and riverbank by paths and roads to Beddgelert.

EAST—From the intersection of the A498 and A4085 in Beddgelert, go S across the bridge on the A498 and turn L along the Afon Colwyn for a few yards and cross the footbridge to a path along the E bank of the Afon Glaswyn. Go R on the first lane to its end by a house and go along the river on grass and rocks to a path along the SE shore of Llyn Dinas. Where the path goes over a small knoll, turn R by a rock cairn to a path slanting up through a deciduous wood. The path comes out to and crosses an open country of small hills, is fairly well trodden and bends E towards high hills. You pass R round a lonely white building (Hafod Owen) and continue E until you reach a road at another white house. Cross the road, pass L of a house and R of another. Climb past Llyn Llagi, keeping L, and go up a moderately steep valley that leads NE from the lake. Turn R about two-thirds of the way up at a large cairn and climb steeply S over the rim of Craig Llyn-Llagi. Pass along the N and E banks of Llyn yr Adar to a low saddle. A path leads SW along what is now seen as a ridge, to Cnicht, whose summit is an easy 1 mile away and 120m above you. Your path goes SE off the ridge over grass and rock, crossing a series of smaller ridges. You pass R of Llyn Cwm-corsiog and descend to old quarry ruins. Walk across the small flat valley towards the roofless buildings to a square cairn, and take a rocky track leading sharp L down Bwlch Cwmorthin to the level land W of Llyn Cwmorthin. Go along the R side of Llyn Cwmorthin, cross the exit stream to a track going down-hill past a waterfall to a road. Walk a short distance to a path L under the cliffs (yellow arrows). In $\frac{1}{2}$ mile cross a narrow-gauge railway line on a footbridge and reach a road. Go L and follow round between the narrow-gauge railway and the standard-gauge railway of British Rail to a bridge L to the A470 at the W end of Blaenau Ffestiniog. The distances are: Llyn Dinas $1\frac{1}{2}$ miles, Llyn Llagi 4 miles, Cnicht saddle 5 miles, Llyn Cwmorthin 7 miles.

8 BEDDGELERT–LLANBERIS
10 miles (16km) 3360ft (1025m) OS 115

Snowdon is by far the most popular mountain to climb in Wales, and it may well be the most popular in Britain. It has many well-defined paths to the summit (W. A. Poucher in *The Welsh Peaks* describes ten) and each path has its own interest. There are four great ridges radiating from the summit, with precipices plunging down to mountain lakes. The view from the top is superb—one of the finest in Britain. On a clear day you can see Ireland, the Isle of Man and Lakeland's Scafell Pike in the far distance. However, your gaze is more likely to be drawn to the nearby ridges, knife-edges, precipices and cwms of the Snowdon massif itself.

Our route takes you by a little-used path from Beddgelert to the long southern ridge between Yr Aran and Snowdon, by that ridge to the busy Snowdon summit with its railway terminus, summit hut and crowds of people, and then by the Llanberis Path to the northern end of our 8 day Walk from Machynlleth. Newcomers to Snowdon will thoroughly enjoy the route as it will display all of Snowdon's charms. Those who have been before may wish for the excitement of other routes but our choice is dictated by the requirements of accommodation and transport at the overnight points and the need for a bad-weather alternative, by which we mean snow or ice on the route. Snowdon's high paths are so well travelled and thus well worn underfoot that mist holds no danger of straying from the way. In this respect, it is perhaps the safest mountain in Wales. However, ice or snow, with the possibility that snow covers ice underneath, may turn a fall into a dangerous downhill slide. And if the chill factor (combination of wind and temperature) is high for the day you climb, you may feel it would be too uncomfortable to be worth it. We therefore provide an alternative lower-level route (section 8a, p133).

Snowdon

While climbing in clouds has little reward, finding yourself above them, as often happens on Snowdon, is a special treat. Then you are on a sea of white with only a few other peaks as neighbours. Under such conditions you may also be lucky enough to see one or both remarkable mountain phenomena: Brocken Spectres and Glories. If you are on a ridge with mist below, you may see a gigantic shadow on the surface of the mist, the Brocken Spectre. It is your shadow and its size is an optical illusion because the shadow is quite close and is your actual size. Under similar conditions a coloured ring may appear around the shadow and this is your Glory.

The way is well marked except for the stretch from near Beddgelert to the south ridge. While the altitude gained is considerable, the gradient in both directions is relatively easy. The footing is good except on the way up from Beddgelert where you are on rough grass and heather.

130

NORTH—Walk NW on the A4085 for 1 mile to a farm lane on the R marked to Perthi Farm. Walk up for ¼ mile to the first farm lane L. Go up through the farmyard of Gwernlas-deg to a track N. Your route for the next 3 miles is mostly pathless. You will climb easily N, then climb fairly steeply W and N under Craig Wen and follow a contour line NE towards the lowest point on the high ridge ahead that runs between Yr Aran and Snowdon.

From Gwernlas-deg you will take the track, going L at the first fork. It soon reduces to a path which finally grows too faint to follow. Keep heading NE, staying above marshy places but below large rocky outcrops on the R under the long ridge of Craig Wen. You pass an old mine at 3 miles and reach a small lake just under the Bwlch Cwm Llan where you join a path coming in from the L. Go R up to the Bwlch (4 miles) and take a well-trodden path N on the long S ridge leading to Snowdon. There are wonderful views L and R off the ridge as you climb. The way is steep at first as you climb Allt Maenderyn. After a drop to the Bwlch Maenderyn, you continue to climb at a steady but not too strenuous rate. At 5 miles the Beddgelert path comes in L and you are now on the Bwlch Main ridge. In ½ mile you reach Snowdon's summit (1085m). Here you will find the summit hut (refreshments and toilets) and the upper terminus of the Snowdon Mountain Railway. You will also have magnificent views of the Glyders and a glimpse of Carnedd Llywelyn to the NE, Moel Siabod to the E, and Mynydd Mawr and Y Garn to the W. Nearer at hand are the four main ridges radiating like sharp-edged spokes from the hub of Yr Wyddfa, Snowdon's true summit. S is the long ridge you have just toiled up, ending in Yr Aran. SE is Lliwedd and NE is Crib-goch; N is the Llanberis ridge. Lakes abound below. Glaslyn and Llyn Llydaw are E, held in the strong embraces of Crib-goch and Lliwedd. To the W are Llyn Cwellyn and half a dozen small lakes.

Leave the summit by the heavily travelled Llanberis path going N just to the E of the railway, with good views R down into Cwm Glas. At Llwybry Mul paths go R down into Cwm Glaswyn and over the Crib-goch ridge and L (the Snowdon Ranger Path). You continue straight ahead and cross under the railway at 6¾ miles. Here good views open up to the W of Moel Cynghorion and Clogwyn-du'r Arddu. At 7½ miles you reach the Halfway House (refreshments) and soon pass under the railway again. Llanberis, Llyn Peris and Llyn Padarn can be seen below. At 9 miles you reach a rough lane. Go R downhill to the first lane on the L (Church Lane). It leads ½ mile to High Street in Llanberis.

SOUTH—Walk SE along High Street in Llanberis to Church Lane R, leading in ½ mile to Victoria Terrace. Go R (SW), pass a roofed noticeboard and begin to climb, with the railway and a stream R (Ceunant Mawr waterfalls here). In ¾ mile the Llanberis path turns L off the lane (sign here). As you gain height, the ridge opens up ahead and you can trace the railway almost to the summit. The highest ground ahead is Garnedd Ugain, ¼ mile away from and only a little lower than Yr Wyddfa, Snowdon's true summit. Look back as you climb, to Llanberis, Llyn Peris and Llyn Padarn. Beyond the Halfway House pass a faint path R and ascend L. After you pass under the railway, you will get good views

Llanberis

to the NE. The ascent steepens until you reach the sharp ridge at Llwyhr y Mul. Snowdon can now been seen ½ mile away and you can gaze down the precipitous cwm enclosed by the Snowdon Horseshoe. Now your way runs close by the railway. The summit hut is slightly below and W of the top. From the hut, head SW down the Bwlch Main ridge on a well-trodden path. Stay on the high ground on the SE side of the ridge, negotiating occasional rocky hummocks on the way. Descend to a small saddle where a path goes R down to the A4085 3 miles from Beddgelert. Our route elects to stay on the ridge all the way to the foot of Yr Aran and to bring you to the main road much nearer Beddgelert. Continue S on the ridge up and over small prominences and steeply down to Bwlch Maenderyn and on down the Allt Maenderyn with a last steep rocky descent to Bwlch Cwm Llan. Follow the R side of a stone wall to a fence and stile at the lowest point of the bwlch. Do not cross the stile but go R on a faint path that skirts the base of a mine tip and cross the dam of the first small lake. From the end of the dam the path disappears except for short faint sections. Ascend slightly and contour SW past an old mine, then descend gradually, staying uphill of marshy ground but below rock outcrops. You will encounter walls and fences en route and may pick up a faint path. You will finally see a track going SW that will take you down to Gwernlas-deg Farm. Go through the farmyard and out of the farm lane past another farm to the A4085. Beddgelert is 1 mile to the L. The distances are: Halfway House 2½ miles, summit hut 4½ miles, Bwlch Cwm Llan 6 miles, Gwernlas-deg Farm 8½ miles.

132

8a BEDDGELERT–LLANBERIS
(Lower Level Alternative)
9 miles (14·5km) 1520ft (460km) OS 115, SNP Snowdon

This route avoids the summit of Snowdon. It goes up a forested valley, by the bed of an abandoned railway and traverses open moorland and a low mountain. Most of the way is fairly well used but without the heavy traffic of the Snowdon paths. Only the way through the forest is at all difficult to follow and only because of the many forest roads and paths. With either of the OS maps and our directions you should have no trouble. If you find yourself bewildered in the forest, simply walk east to the A4085, which runs parallel to the route less than $\frac{1}{2}$ mile away, and follow it between Beddgelert and Rhyd-Ddu.

NORTH—From the junction of the A4085 and the A498 in Beddgelert, walk W on the A498 to the Royal Goat Hotel and go R to the bed of the abandoned Welsh Highland Railway. Here you will find what was once a small marshalling yard: a flat area with the remains of a railway wagon and other pieces of railway equipment. Go NW on the railway bed until you reach a gravel lane crossing under the remains of a railway bridge. Go L on this lane, parallel to a stream on the L until it crosses a track where there are the remains of a bridge across the stream. Go R on this track, once the bed of a branch railway line, and go NW through several cuttings and gates. You pass a caravan park on the R, and will begin to see painted posts (green, yellow and red separated by white; beyond a cross-track the post colours change to blue, red and green separated by white). The posts stop where a side path goes over a stream. You continue straight to a sign to a youth camp ahead and take a track R for 50yd to a marshy footpath L. Confusingly, you are back on a railway bed. Go N until you reach the junction of two forest gravel tracks. Take the one N that is a continuation of your track, built on the railway bed. This ends at another forest track, picnic and parking area, $2\frac{1}{2}$ miles from Beddgelert. Go R a short distance to the A4085 and N about 1 mile to a large car park just S of the small quarrying village of Rhyd-Ddu. This car park was once a substantial station on the railway. From its N end pick up the railway bed, here a firm green track, and follow it for $1\frac{1}{2}$ miles as it winds through green fields. Ahead Llyn Cwellyn will unfold, caught between the steep sides of Mynydd Mawr and Foel-goch. When the lower end of the llyn is on your L, take a grassy path R (N) uphill past the ruins of Tyn-y-ceunant ($5\frac{1}{2}$ miles). You will cross the well-defined Snowdon Ranger Path and reach Bwlch Maes-gym at 6 miles. The pass is unmistakable since the poles of a short section of an abandoned powerline march through it. N of the pass a rocky track slants N gently downhill on the E slope of Foel-goch. As you pass beyond the bulk of Moel Cynghorion, the long NW Llanberis ridge of Snowdon unfolds with the summit in full view. You

will see the trains of the Snowdon Mountain Railway crawling insect-like up the ridge, betrayed by their smoke. On a quiet day their whistles and even their chugging will reach into your valley across the miles of empty air. At 7½ miles you will pass three houses. Take a path R just beyond the last house, go over fields to a footbridge and cross to a path N parallel to the stream. This leads across the Snowdon Railway to a lane. Go L down to a road (Victoria Terrace) and take the first road (Church Lane) L to Llanberis.

SOUTH—Walk SE along the High Street in Llanberis and turn R on Church Lane to Victoria Terrace and go R, continuing ahead on a track when the road ends. Go uphill to the first sharp bend L. Take a path R crossing the railway and running parallel to a stream. Cross the stream at the first footbridge over Afon Arddu to a path L that leads to a track by a group of houses (Brithdir). Go L on the track, going at an easy gradient under Foel-goch, up a long valley between Foel-goch and Moel Cynghorion and over the Bwlch Maes-gym, 3 miles from Llanberis.

Llyn Cwellyn

Here you will have good views of Llyn Cwellyn and Llyn y Gadair and the bulks of Mynydd Mawr and Y Garn. From the pass continue S steeply downhill, cross the Snowdon Ranger Path in ½ mile and reach the level green track of an abandoned railway near the A4085. Go L on this track to the car park S of Rhyd-Ddu on the A4085. Walk S 1 mile on the A4085.

Just beyond the edge of a plantation take a forest track R past a car park and a picnic area to a second forest track L. When it ends at another forest track, continue ahead, now clearly back on the bed of the railway. When you reach a track go R for 50yd to another track. There is a sign R to a youth camp but you go L. You will start passing painted posts (blue, red and green separated by white). At a cross-track these change colour (green, yellow and red separated by white). You pass a caravan park L. When the track crosses another just before a large stream go L on the new track until it passes through an embankment (railway bridge over it here once). Climb the embankment and go R to the Royal Goat Hotel in Beddgelert. The village centre is to the L a short distance on the A498. The distances are: Brithdir $1\frac{1}{2}$ miles, Bwlch Maes-gym 3 miles, Rhyd-Ddu $5\frac{1}{4}$ miles, forest plantation car park $6\frac{1}{2}$ miles.

oldest living inhabitant

CARNEDDAU WALK
North Wales
49 miles (78·75km) 5 days (circuit)

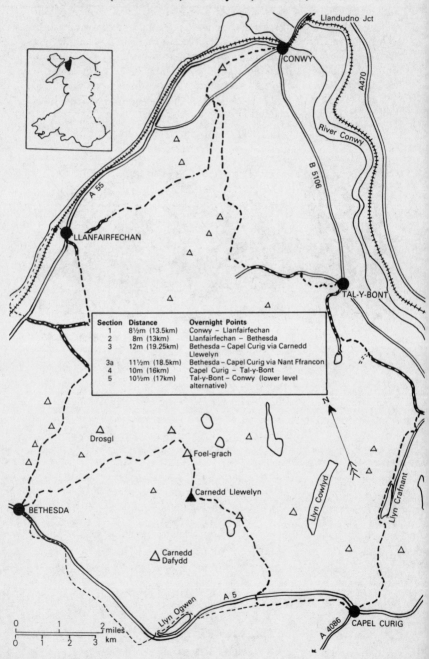

Section	Distance	Overnight Points
1	8½m (13.5km)	Conwy – Llanfairfechan
2	8m (13km)	Llanfairfechan – Bethesda
3	12m (19.25km)	Bethesda – Capel Curig via Carnedd Llewelyn
3a	11½m (18.5km)	Bethesda – Capel Curig via Nant Ffrancon
4	10m (16km)	Capel Curig – Tal-y-Bont
5	10½m (17km)	Tal-y-Bont – Conwy (lower level alternative)

Llandudno Jct

CONWY

A470

River Conwy

B 5106

A 55

LLANFAIRFECHAN

TAL-Y-BONT

N

Drosgl

Foel-grach

Carnedd Llewelyn

Llyn Cowlyd

Llyn Crafnant

BETHESDA

Carnedd Dafydd

Llyn Ogwen

A 5

A 4086

CAPEL CURIG

0   1   2 miles
0 1 2 3 km

ACCOMMODATION
(Conwy has more than 2 hotels and guest houses listed)

Llanfairfechan Chatham House (H) tel (0248) 680138
Myrtlewood (H) tel (0248) 680738
Disguylfa (GH) tel (0248) 681028
Queens House (GH) tel (0248) 680509
Towers Adventure Centre (GH) tel (0248) 680012

Bethesda Ty Pencarrog (PH) Nant Ffrancon tel (0248) 600122
Snowdonia Park (H) Tyn-y-Maes tel (0248) 600548
Maes Caradog Farm (Mrs D. William) tel (0248) 600266

Capel Curig Cobdens Snowdonia (H) tel (06904) 243
Preswylfa (PH) tel (06904) 295
Llugwy (GH) tel (06904) 218
Siabed Villa (GH) tel (06904) 229
Bron Eryri (GH) tel (06904) 240

Tal-y-Bont Olde Bull Inn tel (049269) 508
Y Bedol Inn tel (049269) 501
Lodge Hotel tel (049269) 534

PUBLIC TRANSPORT
Conwy train (British Rail) from Llandudno Jct 1 mile, for Holyhead–Chester freq service Mon–Fri, infreq Sat–Sun, bus (Crosville) Bangor–Llandudno Jct–Chester freq service Mon–Fri, infreq Sat–Sun
Llanfairfechan train (British Rail) Llandudno Jct freq service Mon–Sat, bus (Crosville) Bangor–Conwy–Chester freq service Mon–Sat
Bethesda bus (Crosville Purple) Bangor, Llandegai for bus (Crosville) Bangor–Conwy–Chester freq service Mon–Sat
Capel Curig bus (Crosville Sherpa) Caernarfon 2 r/t dly Mon–Sat, late May–mid Sept, bus (Crosville Sherpa) Llandudno Jct, Conwy 5 r/t dly Mon–Sat, mid July– late Aug
Tal-y-Bont bus (Crosville) Llandudno Jct, freq service Mon–Sat

---

This is a circuit of the wild Carneddau range, the largest group of hills in Snowdonia. The route includes climbs over three peaks, one of which is Carnedd Llewelyn, Wales' third highest mountain. You spend each day on the vast grassy hills and mountains, coming down at night to sea coast and river valleys which surround the range. The circuit includes waterfalls, among them beautiful Aber Falls, stone circles, standing stones and hillforts, the great Norman castle and walled town of Conwy and marvellous views of the valleys and surrounding peaks, the Menai Strait, Anglesey and the sea.

It is a relatively easy Walk with only one strenuous day if you elect to go over Carnedd Llewelyn, and for this we provide a lower-level alternative. As it is a circuit, the start and finish can be at any of the five overnight points but note that Capel Curig only has public transport from mid May to mid September. Local transport is good and you can easily do any segment of the route. The overnight points range from the tiny hamlet of Tal-y-Bont and the small village of Capel Curig through the seaside resort of Llanfairfechan to the town of Conwy with its great castle, town walls and numerous tourist attractions. We recommend that you start and finish at Conwy since it is the easiest to reach by rail or bus; also that you spend an extra day there at the end, unwinding and enjoying its many features of interest.

Besides the OS 1:50,000 series maps selected for each day's walk, the larger-scale OS Outdoor Leisure Maps for Snowdonia National Park (1:25,000) may be used. Either is adequate for route finding. The Outdoor Leisure Maps for the Walk are: Conwy Valley (sections 1, 3, 3a, 4 and 5) and Snowdon (sections 2, 3, 3a), although parts of the route of sections 1 and 2 are not shown.

OVERNIGHT POINTS—Conwy is one of the few medieval walled towns in Europe whose walls are still fully standing. Its most imposing sight is Conwy Castle, built at the same time as the town walls (1283–7) by Edward I. The town is triangular in shape, like a Welsh harp, with one side on the river Conwy. The castle occupies a rock jutting out into the river at one corner of the wall. The area has long been a focal point of Welsh history. The Romans had a large fortified camp up the river and the Welsh princes of the Dark Ages built a stronghold just across the river at Deganwy. A Cistercian Abbey was built here in 1198 but was moved up river when Edward built the castle and town. The river was a formidable barrier which held back the English until Edward's time and drowned or delayed travellers for another five hundred years until the first bridge was built—a suspension bridge by Telford in 1826. There is much to see and do here. The castle should certainly be visited: nearly as imposing as Caernarfon and as handsome as Beaumaris, the beauty of its site cannot be surpassed. The whole north town wall may be walked, the upper end affording a particularly superb view of the town, castle, river and the countryside. The town is visually attractive, with narrow streets and old houses. The oldest is fifteenth-century Aberconwy House, now a National Trust property and open to the public (Apr–Oct dly, Nov–Mar Sat–Sun, 10–5.30). The most elegant house is Plas Mawr, a fine Elizabethan town house and now the headquarters of the Royal Cambrian Academy of Art (similar hours). St Mary's Church, built on the site of the Cistercian Abbey and including some parts of it, is worth a visit. Its spacious churchyard has interesting tombstones, including the grave (protected by an iron screen) of the child celebrated by Wordsworth in 'We are Seven'. The waterfront is a favourite spot and boasts the 'Smallest House in Britain'. From the quay you can take an hour's boat tour of the river Conwy or a deep-sea fishing trip. From the town centre you can also catch a bus to Llandudno (20 minute ride) and visit Great Orme, the mountainous almost-island that juts into the sea, or spend your extra time and money at the many shops of Llandudno. **Llanfairfechan** is a village on the sea where Conwy Bay and the Menai Strait meet. Behind are the high foothills of the Carneddau range, pressing close upon the houses. The old part of the village is built up the side of the steep green valley of the Afon Llanfairfechan, the new part along the seafront. There are two churches. St Mary's stands on a knoll above the village and Christ Church is on the main road at the west end of the village. The latter has a tall spire that is easily seen from far up the hills.

There is a ½ mile Embankment Walk along the sea edge, good for an evening's stroll, with views NW over Lavan Sands to Anglesey and Ynys (Puffin Island or Priestholm) and E to the bluff headland of Penmaenmawr Mount. **Bethesda** is a quarryman's village, the fame of which rests upon the vast Penrhyn slate quarries that cover the east flank of Elider Fawr. The quarry is the largest open-cast slate quarry in the world, covering some 550 acres. The site had been worked as a cottage industry long before the Industrial Revolution but major quarrying was started by Robert Pennant, later Lord Penrhyn, after about 1782. It is still operating and may be visited. The village itself is small, pleasant but unremarkable except for the dominance of the blue–grey colour of the slate, seen in its roofs, walls, stone fences and heaps of debris on the hillside. **Capel Curig** is a mountain hamlet at the junction of the A5 and A4086, a centre for climbers, ramblers and anglers. The A5 is known as the Holyhead Road. It was opened in the early 1800s by Telford and is the inland route to Holyhead, passing through the heart of Snowdonia. Lord Penrhyn built the Royal Hotel here (now the Mountain Adventure Centre) soon after the road replaced a 'dreadful horsepath', and thus opened up the area to visitors. The local church is dedicated to St Curig, from whom the village takes its name. **Tal-y-Bont** is a small village in the Conwy Valley on the B5106. The remains of the Roman fort of Canovium are 1 mile to the N.

1 CONWY–LLANFAIRFECHAN
8½ miles (13·75km) 1100ft (335m) OS 115

Conwy

This is an easy start to the circuit of the Carneddau range and a fine introduction to the mountain uplands of North Wales with their great sweeps of grass and heather and their far views of mountains, rivers and the sea. You climb easily from walled Conwy town to the top of nearby Mynydd y Dref (Conwy Mountain), crowned by an Iron Age hillfort, then by high moorlands past the ancient Druids Circle of stones and down to the coastal village of Llanfairfechan. It is a day for views if the weather is clear, with Conwy and its castle in sight for a long time, the sea and the Menai Strait much at hand below, and some of the high Carneddau peaks peeping at you over the shoulders of their lesser neighbours. Near the end, Llanfairfechan, made tiny by distance, appears at your feet. The way is not difficult to follow, the footing is poor to good.

WEST—Walk NW on the A55 in Conwy. About 100yd after passing through the city wall go L and follow signs to the Mountain Road. When the houses thin out the Mountain Road enters a wood briefly, becomes a dirt track and you climb easily along the S slope of Mynydd y Dref (Conwy Mountain) for $1\frac{1}{2}$ miles. You have a choice of several paths leading R to the ridge of the mountain. Just past a block of white terrace houses, a path slants R uphill through bracken to the ridge. Further on, another path goes back sharply R to the ridge. Once on the ridge you can choose your way, either over the ridge tops or along the landward side on a green track. If you stay on the ridge to the summit (247m), you will reach the ruins of Castell Caer Seion, an Iron Age hillfort. To the unaided eye, the fort consists of an inner oval wall and a lower outer wall and ditch, the latter most in evidence on the seaward side. If the ruins are a bit of a disappointment, the location is not. There is a magnificent panoramic view, N to Great Orme's Head, E to the river Conwy and the town, S to the Carneddau range and W to the Menai Strait, Anglesey and Puffin Island. Below the hillfort on the landward side, just off the green track under the ridge, is a group of hut circles clustered in a small hollow. The circles are merely rings of foundation stones for long-vanished round buildings, probably of wood and turf.

You descend from the summit and reach the dirt Mountain Road. Go R (W) on this track; it swings SW and joins a farm track. Go L to the Sychnant Pass road ($2\frac{1}{2}$ miles from Conwy) and cross to a gate by a footpath sign. Go through and take a green track SE for a 100yd to another track going back R uphill. Take this second track to a wide green field and go S uphill for $\frac{1}{2}$ mile, partly under a powerline, to a dirt track coming downhill from the L and running R (SW) up a valley. You can see the village of Dwygyfylchi and the sea below on the R. The valley ahead is steep-sided and wooded at its lower end but becomes a wide shallow bowl at its upper end. Continue on the track almost to the head of the valley until you see two small reservoirs on the Afon Syrach. Leave the track and cross the stream on a bridge near the reservoirs (4 miles). Head NW across the moorland towards a small building 1 mile away just R of a small hill, keeping to dry ground as much as you can. The map shows other paths across the valley that would be shorter but we were unable to find them. We did find that a lower pathless crossing was very boggy, the river slightly formidable to ford and the longer way by the reservoirs less tiring.

Just by the small building is a sign pointing L to the Druids Circle, Meini Hirion, on Cefn Coch. In $\frac{1}{4}$ mile you will see the stones standing on the skyline, an arresting sight. They are off your direct path but the small climb to them is worth it. At the site you will find a 50ft circle of stones, four of which are large and stand to 4–5ft in height; a dozen others are not much more than rounded boulders lying on the turf. Many have been removed or destroyed. The circle commands only a view E, the other compass points being hidden by nearby hills or the rise of land. If it was an observatory as well as a religious site, it was a fairly limited one. From the circle go W gently downhill across short grass. Llanfairfechan will soon come into view far below, with the Menai Strait and Anglesey beyond. To the S is a broad moorland valley and two ranges of hills, the nearer and lower one dominated by Drosgl (757m), the further one by Foel-fras (942m). The latter is the northern bastion of the Carneddau range proper. When you come to a stone wall (6½ miles) find the gate (you may have strayed off the exact track) and follow a track down through a farm to a lane that soon joins Mount Road (unmarked here). Go R (W) and in a short distance you begin to descend steeply through farmland. Llanfair-fechan will still be far below you. Go down through the village until you reach the A55 at a set of traffic lights. The hotels, guest houses and B&Bs are to the R along the A55 or ahead along the waterfront.

Llanfairfechan

EAST—From the traffic lights on the A55 in Llanfairfechan go SE uphill. Take a R fork past the post office and follow the signs L to Mount Road. This road leads you, fairly steeply at first, between houses and then through farmland for 1½ miles. Shortly after the road levels out, high above the village, you will pass the entrance to a Holiday Association centre. Take the lane going uphill just R of this entrance. This leads you past a quarry entrance on the L and through a farm to a track running E easily uphill to open moorland. The track continues E, less well defined, passing L of a high hill (Moelfre) over fairly level ground. You pass an orange sign with '19' on it (digression to Druids Circle to the R), and continue E to a sign pointing back to the circle. Go R past a small building and head SE on the driest ground across the Syrach Valley towards two small reservoirs at its head. Cross the Afon Syrach on a bridge near the reservoirs and go NE down the valley, picking up a dirt track that runs roughly parallel to the stream. After passing a farmhouse on the L, leave the track where it bends sharply to the R and follow a powerline over a small rise and go downhill. When a wood comes into view ahead, head

141

for it by any convenient path and go L along its edge to a gate and the Sychnant Pass road. Cross to a lane opposite and, in ¼ mile, go R at a footpath sign to a dirt track (Mountain Road) that will lead you down to the A55 at the outskirts of Conwy. Go R for the town centre. If you choose to walk on the ridge, take one of the tracks L from the Mountain Road but be sure to return to it before the ridge reaches a wood. The distances are: Druids Circle sign 3½ miles, Sychnant Pass 6 miles.

2 LLANFAIRFECHAN–BETHESDA
8 miles (13km) 1800ft (550m) OS 115

This is an easy walk, partly on open moorland, partly in woods and farmland. You will pass Rhaeadr-Fawr (Aber Falls), with its 53m drop into the valley of the Afon Goch. The challenge of the walk is the route finding over the high moorland as the path is faint to non-existent in places. There is little danger of getting lost, however, only in being slightly and temporarily misplaced. You have excellent views of Conwy Bay, the island of Anglesey and Ynys (Puffin Island or Priestholm) at Anglesey's north end. You also have a choice, as part of the walk, of going along the shore of Conwy Bay. The day we walked we started well before breakfast and arrived in Bethesda in time for a late 'elevenses'. Parked outside the local café was a long line of children's push chairs. Inside, cheerful mums were having their morning coffee with the help of their active charges. The town seemed to be more than holding its own. The walk is not strenuous except for the climb up from the sea and the footing is good except for a few boggy places.

SOUTHWEST—Walk SW on the A55 from Station Road in Llanfair-fechan to the next road L, marked to a cemetery and golf course. Take this road uphill past the golf course and at the next fork (½ mile) keep R on

time out

142

Llannerch Road. Soon a stony track with a footpath sign goes L. Go 100yd along this track and turn L again, ignoring a second footpath sign pointing ahead. You will be on what was once a fine carriage road, but is now a rough track, that leads through trees into open farmland. Before you reach a farmhouse, go R uphill across a field to a fence and stile alongside an evergreen forest. Cross to a wide dirt path going downhill through the forest a short distance to a dirt track at the forest edge. Go L uphill to the first kissing-gate on the R and go through it into a field. You will see a stone pillar a few yards further on (Roman pillar on a modern cement base?). From the gate, take a bearing over the pillar and go on this line up through a thin deciduous wood and fields to a gate at the top of the fields (2 miles). Near the gate a rough track runs L and R. This is the remains of a Roman road running between the Roman forts of Canovium on the river Conwy and Segontium near Caernarfon. Go R on this road. It soon turns S along a high stone wall and you reach the end of a lane. Go steeply downhill on this lane to a fork (3 miles) (Bont Newydd) and go L along the E side of the Afon Rhaeadr Fawr. The lane becomes a gravel track ending at a small house. Take a worn path round the house and on to the Aber Falls. From the house, look ahead to the skyline S. You will see a definite saddle cut by the Afon Gam. This is your route after leaving the falls. Once the falls are reached ($4\frac{1}{4}$ miles), cross the stream below them, go over a stile and work your way W, first along a stone wall and then a fence to a stile by the Afon Gam. You will pass by a smaller falls. Cross the stile and ford the stream to its W bank. Follow it, at first near its bank but gradually moving high above it as the valley narrows. Continue SW after the stream peters out to the saddle you saw earlier ($5\frac{1}{2}$ miles). Do not waste time looking for the paths shown on the OS map but head SW, passing L of a distinctive peak (Gyrn). Beyond, you will pick up a path leading down towards Bethesda. It passes L of Llefn and Moel Faban and reaches a road running down to your destination, Bethesda.

There is an alternative route between Llanfairfechan and Bont Newydd, partly by a good path along the shore W from Llanfairfechan. You reach the path from Station Road and follow it for $2\frac{1}{2}$ miles. About $\frac{1}{4}$ mile after crossing the Afon Rhaeadr Fawr, you strike a road. Go L under the railway to the A55 at Aber. Dog-leg L to a road going SE uphill and join your regular route at Bont Newydd. The alternative is about 1 mile longer but is easier walking.

NORTHEAST—In Bethesda, go E off the A5 on a road just N of the Post Office. Turn L in $\frac{1}{4}$ mile uphill past a grocery shop and continue beyond two groups of houses straight uphill, coming out on the open moorland through two kissing gates. A faint track goes NE, passing to the R of Moel Faban and Lefn. You may lose the track here but head directly for Gyrn and pass to its R on any contour. From Gyrn head NE. Ahead you will soon see the steep face down which the Aber Falls plunge (but the falls will not be visible) and beyond it a large forest. You will pass the highest point without noticing it but, as the ground begins to slope away before you, search for the beginning of the Afon Gam. Go down its NW bank, first high above it and then near it until it passes under a fence. Cross the stream and go over a stile. Turn R along the fence and then along a stone wall to Aber Falls. Cross the river just below the falls and take a worn path down to a gravel track and then a lane. Continue downhill past two side lanes on the R (the second lane goes to a car park and toilets). Take the third lane (Bont Newydd) and go fairly steeply uphill to the end of the metalled surface. Go L over a stile on to the moorland and follow a high stone wall to a track coming in from the R under Foelgapol (Roman road). Go L on this track and when it turns sharp R, leave it and go through two gates where stone walls join to make a 'T' and go NE downhill across a field. Ahead, on the opposite slope, you will see an evergreen forest. Head for the midpoint of its W edge, passing through a thin deciduous wood en route. There is what appears to be the stub of a Roman column standing about 2m high in the field near the evergreen forest and just beyond is a kissing-gate in a stone wall. Go through the gate and turn L downhill on a dirt track between the wall and the forest. Take the first wide dirt track going R uphill through the forest. It leads you into the open and a stile takes you into a field. Go downhill towards a farmhouse. From the L of the house take a faint track N. You will find yourself on the rough remains of what was once a fine carriage road. By a footpath sign go R for 100yd to a road and R on the road down to the A55 in Llanfairfechan. All accommodation is to the R. The distances are: Aber Falls 3¾ miles, Roman road 6 miles.

Christ Church

3 BETHESDA–CAPEL CURIG
12 miles (19.25km) 2950ft (900m) OS 115

Penrhyn quarries

This is an exciting day over two of the Carneddau peaks, both above 900m in height. It includes Carnedd Llewelyn, the highest member of the range and the third highest in Wales, just slightly lower than Snowdon. The route also includes walking along the edge of the great precipices of Craig-yr-Ysfa and negotiating the airy ridge to Penyrhelgi-du. The views from the ridges and summits are superb. The Menai Strait, Anglesey and the Irish Sea are to the northwest and west; to the southwest and south stretch the Glyder range, while to the east and southeast are the outliers of the main Carneddau range and the vast amphitheatre of Cwm Eigiau.

The walk is fairly strenuous but rewarding. In clear weather it can be done by anyone reasonably fit. A few stretches require mild scrambling but it is otherwise not difficult. However, Carnedd Llewelyn should not be attempted if the mountain tops are in the clouds as its summit is flat and featureless and the several paths from it not well marked with cairns. Once below its summit, however, the way is easy to follow. South is over steep but sharply marked terrain and the way north is well trodden, reasonably well marked with cairns, with safe grassy slopes west and a refuge hut for emergencies. We have included a low-level route via the Pass of Nant Ffrancon in case you feel the weather is too bad to venture on the heights (section 3a, p148). The footing is good.

SOUTHEAST—Take the first road (Penybryn Road) E off the A5 N of Bethesda post office and walk uphill to the cluster of houses marked 'Gerlan' on the OS map. Take the only lane uphill from Gerlan. It soon becomes a track ending in sheep pens (1 mile). Go through a gate in a stone wall out to the moorland and turn R on an old track by the wall leading E up the Afon Caseg Valley. The stream is visible on your R perhaps $\frac{1}{8}$ mile away. The head of the valley is cut prominently by its tributary, the Afon Wen, and your course is up this slope, keeping L of the stream, to the saddle between Garnedd-uchaf and Foel-grach. The old track in the valley soon becomes faint and difficult to follow. The driest route is to stay L and well uphill of the stream on a long, low mound running up the lower part of the valley. As the way steepens, you will reach another faint track at $3\frac{1}{2}$ miles running R to old sheep pens by the stream. Go R on this track. You can make your way from it to the saddle anywhere L of the stream but you should gradually move towards the stream as you gain height and reach and follow it near the top of the rise. The slope you will be walking on is partly grassy, partly broken rocks, and is steep but never difficult. To your R (S) the crags of Yr Elen will draw your attention. To the SW is the distant cone of Elider Fawr. When the stream peters out, continue in the same direction (E). As the slope lessens a faint path begins. It soon intersects a well-trodden path running along the saddle ($4\frac{1}{2}$ miles). Go R (S) and climb gently for $\frac{1}{2}$ mile to the summit of Foel-grach (974m). There is a mountain refuge hut on its N side. From the summit there are good views of the N part of the Carneddau range rising from the moorlands. Continue S along a broad grassy ridge by a well-worn path with some cairns, and climb the rocks of Carnedd Llewelyn to its flat summit (1062m, 6 miles). In clear weather there is a magnificent panoramic view from the top. The most dramatic sector is to the S and SW, with the serrated ridge of the Glyder range dominated by the dagger-like N side of Tryfan. Snowdon looms in the background just R of Tryfan. Nearer at hand is the long ridge of Carnedd Dafydd, and NW is the shapely peak of Yr Elen. Beyond Anglesey, the Irish Sea stretches from W to N. In very clear weather it is possible to see the Wicklow Mountains of Ireland and the Isle of Man.

From Llewelyn descend, steeply at times, first bearing slightly SE over the summit rocks, then more S over the hump of Penywaun-wen and down along an invigorating knife-edge to the saddle between Llewelyn and Penyrhelgi-du, an easy scramble. On your L are the precipices of Craig-yr-Ysfa and you pass several near-vertical chimneys that yawn menacingly. At the saddle (7 miles) you can go one of three ways: R down to a road from Ffynnon Llugwy reservoir and so out to the A5; ahead up to the top of Penyrhelgi-du and down its S buttress to the A5; or take an almost level path across the stony W face of Penyrhelgi-du to the S buttress. The buttress itself is broad, grassy and gently descending. As you come down, look ahead below to the A5 and the river running parallel to it (Afon Llugwy). Head for the A5 at a point between a small group of buildings and a group of trees. As you come off the buttress you will cross a stone wall and reach a leat. Look for two bridges over the leat, probably to your R and cross rough grassland to Talybraich Farm where you go R out to the A5 ($9\frac{1}{2}$ miles). Cross to a boggy path and two stone-slab bridges to a gate in a clump of trees and turn L on the old Holyhead road, now a green track, running parallel to the A5. It is $2\frac{1}{2}$ miles to Capel Curig.

Craig-yr-Ysfa

NORTHWEST—At the junction of the A5 and A4086 in Capel Curig go L around the post office and general stores, by the public toilets to a gate and lane running N and then W parallel to the A5 along the S bank of the Afon Llugwy. It becomes a gravel track and than a grassy one. At $2\frac{1}{2}$ miles from Capel Curig turn R through a clump of trees at an ornamental iron gate and go over two stone-slab bridges to the A5. Cross the road to a National Trust signpost for Tal-y-braich and a footpath sign pointing up a rough farm track. Go several 100yd up the track to a second footpath sign and go L uphill across fields to the grassy S buttress of Penyrhelgi-du. Near the summit watch for a narrow path branching to the L. This keeps almost level across the W side of the mountain to a saddle. You can, however, continue to the summit of Penyrhelgi-du and descend steeply NW down to this saddle.

From the saddle ascend NW to Carnedd Llewelyn, then N to Foel-grach. Descend N on the ridge path for about $\frac{1}{2}$ mile to the midpoint between Foel-grach and Garnedd-uchaf and take any faint path L (W). If you are unable to find the path, judge when you have gone about $\frac{1}{2}$ mile, turn L and walk over the ridge lip until you spot Afon Wen and correct your route. The slope is safe to descend almost anywhere between Foel-grach and Garnedd-uchaf. Descend by the Afon Wen's N bank to the floor of the valley and go W, keeping the river, now the Afon Caseg, $\frac{1}{8}$ mile or so on your L. You will reach a farm lane that will take you down into Bethesda. The distances are: Carnedd Llewelyn 6 miles, Foel-grach 7 miles.

3a BETHESDA–CAPEL CURIG
(Lower Level Alternative)
11½ miles (18.5km) 480ft (150m) OS 115

This alternative route avoids climbing the peaks of our main route and is to be preferred when the tops are in clouds or the temperature and wind combine to make upland walking unpleasant or dangerous. The way is mostly by an eighteenth-century road which was a packhorse path before that and is said to have been a Roman road even earlier. It goes through the steep-sided Pass of Nant Ffrancon, lined with glacier-made hanging valleys of the Glyders range, and down the valley of the Afon Llugwy.
SOUTHWEST—Walk S on the A5 from the post office in Bethesda, cross the Afon Llafar at its confluence with the Afon Gwen and take the first road R over the Afon Gwen (Pont Twr). Go L immediately on a lane and footpaths along what is now the Afon Ogwen, to the next bridge and cross back to the A5. Go R for ¼ mile to another bridge, cross to Dolawen and follow a path S to the Old Bethesda Road, running along the W side of the Afon Ogwen. This rejoins the A5 at Pont-y-benglog (5¼ miles) (see the arch under the present bridge, said to be Roman). Dog-leg L on the A5 to a path running along the N and E sides of Llyn Ogwen and cross the A5 back to the old Road (6½ miles). Follow this S to Capel Curig.

4 CAPEL CURIG – TAL-Y-BONT
10 miles (16km) 2250ft (685m) OS 115

This is a fascinating ramble through the eastern foothills of the Carneddau range. It goes between two tiny communities, unalike in both setting and character. Capel Curig is a true mountain hamlet set at a crossroads, with views of high peaks on all sides, and is a mountaineering centre. Tal-y-Bont is a little-visited community of a few houses, an inn, church and shop. The fertile river bottom of the Vale of Conwy is to the E and hill farms in the foothills of the Carneddau range are to the W. On your way between these two hamlets you will walk through all kinds of countryside: a mountain pass, high moorland, woods and hill farms. You will go along the forested edge of beautiful Llyn Crafnant and later pass under great waterpipes, cross leats, travel an abandoned railway line and see an inclined railway still intact. It is a walk to test your route-finding ability as the way is intricate in places. However, you are never far from roads and houses. The footing varies from poor to excellent, a variety you may not appreciate.
NORTH—From the intersection of the A5 and A4086 in Capel Curig go E over a stile to a footpath past the church and then a knoll on the R. Look back and see Snowdon. Pass through a small wood above farms

Capel Curig

(youth hostel can be seen R downhill and Moel Siabod to the S). After 1 mile the path swings N and you climb easily along the Nant y Geuallt. At 2 miles take a L fork and descend into a narrow valley at head of Llyn Crafnant. At the Tynach Climbing Club building go a short way NE and then L on a grassy track to a stony road running parallel to the lake (3 miles). Go L through a gate marked 'Hendre' (teas once served here and they may be again). From Hendre you have a choice of a high path through the wood or a low path along the NW shore. These paths join about midway along the lake and you follow the shoreline to its NE end where you again have a choice of routes. The simplest way is to cross the bridge and go L down the road to Gelli (signposted) where you rejoin our preferred route which avoids the road. This way, instead of crossing the bridge, go over a fence into rough pasture and head NE above the stream and road. Make for a telegraph pole on the hillside and from it go NE along the contour through a short boggy stretch to a distinct track worn by pony hooves. Take this track through fields with gates to a lane, and go L uphill through a farmyard to a gate and stile. From here a path goes along an open hillside in front of a caravan and pink-washed cottage. There are good views ahead and you will see the abandoned workings of a large quarry on the hillside opposite. Behind you there is a spectacular view of Llyn Crafnant with Moel Siabod towering in the distance. The path runs parallel to telegraph poles and ends at a road (4½ miles). Go R a short distance until the first switchback where you leave the road and continue ahead through a gate to a path into a larch and pine wood. Take the middle of a three-way fork, and at the next fork go R along a stream to a road. Turn L a short distance to another gate L just before a white house marked 'Gelli' (the alternative way from Crafnant joins here). Go through a gate up the hill and now pick up yellow discs. The way twists and turns, so keep a sharp eye for the signs. Go over a stile into a farmyard (Gelli Newydd) and follow its access track to a lane (5½ miles). Go L uphill for about ¼ mile. Shortly after the lane turns sharp L, go R on another lane through a gate. You are soon in the open on a shoulder of Cefn Cyfarwydd. Below is the Vale of Conwy with the river Conwy snaking along the valley floor. To the L is Carnedd Llewelyn, Foel-grach and Foel-fras. When you begin to descend into the valley of the Afon Ddu, on

149

its opposite slope you will see the black line of a huge pipe running along the ground, carrying water from the Llyn Cowlyd reservoir to furnish power to the aluminium works at Dolgarrog. The lane deteriorates into a track, swings W and you reach a footpath sign nailed to a large oak by some dilapidated farm buildings. Go R downhill to a footbridge, following the yellow markers on the rocks. Cross and slant L uphill (no markers, over what is almost a bridge, and follow the little stream that flows under it uphill to a stile R. Cross and go L along the edge of a field, through two gates and go uphill over a leat (choice of two bridges here) to a rough track above. You may be tempted to walk along the grassy leat wall but it soon disappears into a tunnel. Go R on the track and you will discover that it is the abandoned bed of a railway. You will find wooden sleepers cast up on the side, then iron rails, and finally, after you pass under two large pipes, you will find rails still in place and a small building that once housed the railway engine (8 miles). By a second small building is an inclined railway with its rails still in place. This is all very exciting to railway buffs or amateur industrial archeologists. The two railways were built around 1905 for transporting equipment and material to build the several reservoirs in the Carneddau range and to bring up the great pipe sections that criss-cross the countryside. Continue along the railway bed, now alongside a leat. After you see another large pipe below to the R, you will spot a bridge across the stream beyond (Pont Newydd over Afon Porthllwyd, 8 miles). You can either head directly downhill for the bridge as soon as you see it, crawling under the pipeline en route, or continue ahead to the lane coming down from Cocdty Reservoir. As you cross the Afon Porthllwyd, you might pause a moment and think of the terrible night of 3 November 1923 when the dam of Llyn Eigiau broke and sent a wall of water rushing down the valley of the Afon Porthllwyd through the village of Dolgarrog far below. Luckily, most of the villagers were at a cinema safely out of the way or the loss of life (16 people) would have been much greater. Cross the bridge and go 2 miles through high farms down to Tal-y-Bont. The last $\frac{1}{2}$ mile is a 1:4 gradient, hard on brakes and hard on knees.

SOUTH—S of the bridge over the Afon Dulyn on the B5106 in Tal-y-Bont takes a lane W for 2 miles to Pont Newydd. Cross the bridge and in several 100yd go sharp L on a rough farm track that leads you past an

Llyn Crafnant

inclined railway round the base of Penardda. Soon after the track swings SW, leave it and go downhill over a leat to a sheepfold. Go through two gates to a field, down its R side to a stile and then straight down through a wood and over a footbridge. Follow yellow markers uphill to a farm track and go L. It soon becomes a lane. Go L at a T-junction downhill to Gelli Newydd (signposted) and go R through a farmyard to a marked path. Follow the markers down to a road and go R 1¼ miles to Llyn Crafnant. Cross the bridge at the NE end of the Llyn and walk SW along the shore of the lake to a path. At Hendre go L on a stony track for a short distance to a path S that leads in about 2 miles to Capel Curig. The distances are: Pont Newydd 2 miles, Gelli Newydd Farm 4½ miles, Llyn Crafnant 6¼ miles.

5 TAL-Y-BONT–CONWY
10½ miles (17km) 1600ft (490m) OS 115

This is a moorland walk that climbs out of the Vale of Conwy to the east slope of the Carneddau range. Once on the moor the way is mostly on grassy tracks and paths high above the Conwy Valley to Sychnant Pass and by Mynydd y Dref (Conwy Mountain) to Conwy. There are waterfalls, standing stones, an Iron Age fort, a section of Roman road and a disused quarry to look at on the way. There are constant views east of the woods and farms of the Conwy Valley and the hills beyond, and long glimpses west of the interior hills and valleys of the Carneddau range. The going is easy, the route not difficult to follow. The footing is generally good and reasonably dry.

NORTH—Walk N from the Y Bedol Inn in Tal-y-Bont on the B5106 to the first road L. In a 100yd, past a gate L marked 'Rivulet', go through a farm gate L to a track. When the track turns R, go straight ahead through a kissing-gate to a path along the N bank of the Afon Dulyn. You now have a delightful stroll along the stream as it tumbles down through a narrow wooded valley. After the last stile before a foot-bridge, ½ mile from Tal-y-Bont, go R (N) uphill to a muddy path

151

between high hedges. Follow the path N. Soon after a gate L, take an ancient stile L over the hedge to a field and head NW a short distance to farm buildings. L of the buildings take a track N past a second set of buildings and go down a lane to the first stile on the L. Cross to a field and go uphill W and then NW over a second stile. Follow a faint green track to a gate and a lane by a water treatment plant $1\frac{1}{2}$ miles from Tal-y-Bont. Go L uphill, first through farmland and then moorland for $2\frac{1}{2}$ miles and at a fork go sharp R on a track below a single white house (Cae Coch). Stop here and note the continuation of the lane you were just on, veering W, and the track you are now on, going E. This is the old Roman road between Canovium and Segontium that you met briefly in section 2 (p143). Unfortunately, you leave it almost immediately on a track L among small farm buildings. This track soon swings NE and you climb easily along a wall for 1 mile to a gate and stile. Cross and contour (no path) under a steep slope L, passing L of a knob of rock (Caer Bach). Go NW uphill, passing Tal y Fan quarry, to a track N of the quarry ($5\frac{1}{2}$ miles). You will have good views ahead to Conwy Mountain and much of the intervening route, as well as a view NW into the valley of the Afon Syrach. Go R on the track; it swings N and you skirt a long stone wall for about 2 miles. You will pass two standing stones, a substantial one near the quarry. The track joins another track near a small lake (Gwarn Engen). At the lake take a path along its W side, over a stile to a track leading N to the road at Sychnant Pass ($8\frac{1}{2}$ miles). Follow the **EAST** directions of the Conwy–Llanfairfechan section (p141) over Conwy Mountain to Conwy.

Conwy

SOUTH—Follow the **WEST** direction of the Conwy–Llanfairfechan section to Sychnant Pass (p139). Cross the road and go through a gate to a green track to the S. Soon after passing an underground cistern take a stile over a stone wall L of a hill ahead. Pass R of a small lake to a track S. It soon forks. Go R uphill to a second fork and go L on a track S along a long wall to a quarry. Take the track through the quarry. It peters out beyond the quarry but you continue S along the hill slope, passing R of a rock knob, to a stone wall with a gate and stile. Go over stile to a track running

SW gently downhill along a stone wall, to a lane by a white house (Cae Coch). Go L downhill on the lane for 2½ miles. By a water treatment plant go R through a gate into a field and slant downhill on a green track to a stile, across a second field to another stile and lane. Go R, pass R of two sets of farm buildings (lane becomes a track). Slant down through another field, go over a stile to a path between hedges and go to the Afon Dulyn. Go L on a path along the stream to a path and track L leading to a road. Tal-y-Bont is to the R. The distances are: Sychnant Pass 2 miles, quarry 5 miles, Cae Coch 6½ miles.

NOTES

Note A Accommodation and Public Transport

In our walking we have found it difficult to find out what is available by way of both accommodation and public transport for the out-of-the-way places in which you will be walking. The following notes may therefore be helpful to you.

Accommodation

If you stay on the beaten tourist track in any country, a call to your travel agent will usually suffice to secure accommodation. However, in our Walks you will be well away from the tourist paths (this is one of their charms) and only a few of the overnight points have accommodation listed with travel agents. Thus, that easy solution is effectively denied you. To help you, here is a distillation of our experience and what we have gathered from tourist departments, innkeepers and fellow travellers along the way.

1 FINDING WHAT IS AVAILABLE

Easiest for you is a list of what is potentially available. Unfortunately, there is no single complete list for all of Wales. The Wales Tourist Board publishes two annual volumes: *Wales, Where to Stay* and *B&B in Wales, Bed & Breakfast Guide* (available at a charge from The Wales Tourist Board, Brunel House, Cardiff CF2 1UY, Wales). Although these list some 4000 places, they probably miss half of those potentially available and entirely miss those for many of the more remote overnight points. Other more local accommodation lists are available but are not easy to procure at a distance.

We have therefore included at the beginning of each Walk a list of accommodation for the overnight points which have two or fewer hotels and guest houses listed in the 1983 *Wales, Where to Stay*. Therefore, if the overnight point is not given, you will find three or more hotels and guest houses listed in that publication. The names of the accommodation we list come from a variety of sources and there is no certainty that they will still be open when you call. As a rule of thumb, hotels (H) are most likely to be available year after year, guest house (GH) less likely, while B&Bs or private homes (PH) come and go at the pleasure of their owners. We provide addresses and telephone numbers so that you can readily find out if the accommodation is still available and, more timely, if they have beds

155

free for your desired date(s). If you draw a blank in your enquiries for those overnight points with little listed accommodation, we have found a letter to the local postmaster (or mistress) (with an SAE) sometimes works. Also if you find one accommodation full, you can ask that establishment to refer you to another and they almost always will.

2 SECURING ACCOMMODATION

We feel that it is absolutely essential to confirm reservations before you set out. You are not the casual car traveller that you may have been before, easily able to cover many miles in search of lodgings (and in Wales the car traveller lacking accommodation may well have to do that in the summer). Many of our overnight points have a limited number of beds, making it especially likely that they will be fully booked. Start finding out what is available and make reservations well in advance of your trip — perhaps a month if you live in Britain and at least two months if you live abroad. We find the instructions in *Wales, Where to Stay* hard to improve on, so with the permission of the Wales Tourist Board, we quote from that publication:

> When making a written enquiry please always enclose a stamped addressed envelope to insure a speedy reply to your enquiry. In your enquiry you should always state:
>
> 1 The dates for which you wish to book as well as any alternatives.
> 2 The number of people in your party.
> 3 Any special requirements that you may need, ie terms for children, special diets, facilities for pets.

> If the establishment can supply you with the accommodation required you should always confirm your definite requirement in writing as soon as possible to the establishment, enclosing any booking deposit that may be required.
>
> Guests who have made prior bookings at establishments and who intend to arrive late can help by phoning the establishment well in advance and advising the establishment of the intended time of their arrival.
>
> When you make a booking and accept the conditions of that booking, bear in mind you may be entering into a legally binding contract with the proprietor of the establishment which might entitle the proprietor of accommodation to compensation if you fail to take up the accommodation.
>
> Accordingly, if you have to change your travel plans and cancel a booking, remember that it is in your interest to advise the management or owner immediately.

We would add that it is also a courtesy to inform the establishment if you cannot take up the accommodation.

The Wales Tourist Board operates a bed-booking service in its tourist information centres. However, you must go in person to a centre and their listing is only for their local area. We have stressed that you should have secured accommodation in advance but, if you do not, the bed-booking service may be useful to you. We indicate in the Index the overnight points that have tourist information centres with bed-booking service.

We learned the hard way that accommodation listed for a particular place may be some miles from the town or village centre. This is especially true for farmhouses but guest houses and even hotels may be at a distance. We have noted this in our listing where the distance is greater than $\frac{1}{2}$ mile. For accommodation other than those we list our advice is that you ask for the precise location when you telephone or write. The added distance may be more than you are willing to undertake at the end of a day's walk. However, accommodation distant from the town centre may sometimes be conveniently on your route.

A number of overnight points have youth hostels in or very near them. We have indicated in the Index which overnight point has a hostel *which also serves meals*. You may like to share their somewhat austere but always friendly and low-cost accommodation. If you have been a resident of England or Wales for more than a year you can stay at these hostels by purchasing Guest Passes without joining the Youth Hostel Association (YHA) (international regulation). However, we encourage you to join the YHA (Trevelyan House, 8 St Stephan's Hill, St Albans, Herts AL1 2DY. If you use the hostels for more than three nights a membership is also cheaper than the Guest Passes.

Public Transport

The Walks have each been selected so that the start and finishing points both have public transport facilities available. With very few exceptions, the intermediate overnight points can also be reached by public transport, making for great flexibility in your selection of a walking tour. For each overnight point, the type of transport available and its nearest connection to Wales' major transport network are given on the pages which introduce each Walk. Generally, the frequency (eg 5 r/t dly) and the days of the week operating (eg Mon–Fri) are also given. The name of the transport company is also given; the telephone numbers to dial for up-to-date information are listed at the end of this Note. You may also obtain detailed and up-to-date information at tourist information centres, all railway stations, bus terminals and most bus stops. Wales still has a well-developed railway network which provides a fast, comfortable service to or near most of our Walks.

Some useful telephone numbers are given on the next page.

157

Crosville   Chester 381515
National Welsh   Abergavenny 3299 Mon–Sat 9am–5.30pm
Richard Bros   Newport 820751
                    Moylgrove 205
Bala Lake Railway   Llanuwchyllyn 666
                    Bala 520266
Talyllyn Railway   Tywyn 710472
Brecon Mountain Railway   Merthyr Tydfil 4854

Note B   Route Finding

We have chosen our routes and written our route information bearing in mind people who may never have walked on anything other than clearly marked and well-defined paths. Because our routes are rarely signposted and because the way is sometimes indistinct, a minimum knowledge of the use of maps and a compass is desirable. If you can read a car map, can follow instructions in cookery recipes and can take a few minutes to make friends with a compass, you can gain this minimum knowledge from our Note. For most of our routes only our guidebook and the maps we recommend are necessary, but on occasion you will need the compass in order to distinguish approximate directions relative to north.

1   MAPS AND MAP READING

We recommend and use the new Ordnance Survey Landranger maps 1:50,000 series ($1\frac{1}{4}$in to the mile or 2cm per kilometre). We also use, where pertinent, the OS Outdoor Leisure Maps 1:25,000 series ($2\frac{1}{2}$in to the mile or 4cm per kilometre) (Snowdonia and Brecon Beacons National Parks). There are other 1:25,000 series maps (OS Pathfinder Series) but we do not specify these. We find the 1:50,000 series maps completely adequate and a nice balance between the walker's need for detail and for economy of load and cost (the Pathfinder 1:25,000 Series necessitates up to four times the number of maps per Walk). Assuming that everyone is familiar with road maps in this car age, the OS maps will be strange only in their symbols and their use of contour lines to show the height of the land above sea level. You will pick up the meaning of most of the map symbols through encountering them as you go along. Their meaning is given in the right-hand corner or on the bottom edge of each map. Walkers, of course, are most interested in the footpaths (single-dashed black or red lines, dotted red lines and a special red symbol for old roads used as paths, red signifying in England and Wales a public right of way). Dotted black lines are not footpaths but electoral boundaries (civil parish or equivalent), a confusion we once fell into.

The contour lines on the map are intended to display the terrain relief, that is, to show how the land humps up. These lines are easy to understand but difficult to use. They are lines joining points on the earth's surface that are at the same elevation above sea level. Somewhat confusingly, on the first issue of the new OS maps (1:50,000), their height above sea level, printed occasionally along the contour lines, is in metres but their vertical interval, the incremental height between two adjacent lines, may be 50ft. This is because the contour lines of the first set of 1:50,000 maps were drawn from the older 1in maps, which used that vertical interval. We should mention that the heights of the various peaks and summits are given here and in the 1:50,000 series maps in metres.

Now to explain how to use the contour lines. A moment's reflection will make you realise that when the lines are shown close together, the land is steep, and when far apart, it is relatively flat. Be very careful to spot places where the contour lines disappear altogether. This is not because the Ordnance Survey has become fed up with drawing them — rather, the terrain has become perpendicular! Take special care near such places.

The problem is to visualise the actual earth surface from the map representation. Some people seem born with this ability, most are not. Everyone, however, can learn quite a bit by comparing the map and the land while travelling along. Armchair travelling does not seem to help much — we are constantly surprised by the 'seen' terrain as compared to the terrain visualised when just studying the map. But once in the field, comparing real and map features makes the contour lines come alive.

The terrain features mentioned in the text and the way they are spelt corresponds to the OS 1:50,000 series maps (the spelling may differ from other maps and even from local usage) or to familiar topographical features. A glossary of the Welsh map features and corresponding English meaning is given on page 167. A short glossary of common features is given here for the benefit of those to whom the words may be unfamiliar.

Bwlch or pass   a low point on a ridge or mountain range.
Contouring   moving across a hillside without gaining or losing elevation.
Cwm   a valley, generally in the mountains.
Hafod   summer dwelling, now generally in ruins, occupied temporarily by persons watching over grazing animals.
In spate   refers to streams and rivers, when unusually high water occurs from rain or melting snow, which may make it dangerous to cross at such times (see p164).
Leat   a canal carrying water from or between reservoirs.
Llyn   a lake.
Shoulder   a rounded, steep but not precipitous projection from a hill or mountain.
Rhiw   hill, slope or a track slanting across a slope.

Types of compass There is a wide variety of compasses on the market and a similar range of prices. *Any* compass is adequate, However, we recommend a fluid-damped compass, in which the needle moves in a clear liquid, as an undamped needle will quiver annoyingly when hand held. Compasses come with additional features such as a luminous dial for use at night, a protractor base to aid direct use on a map, a sighting device for more accurately determining the bearing of a distant object, and several methods of carrying (wrist strap, neck cord). They all add to the weight and price. We feel the most useful additional feature is the protractor base. If you want this aid, the least expensive one sold for orienteering will be quite good enough.

Reading the compass Compasses are almost all marked in *points* and *degrees* (a few engineering compasses are in degrees only, a few old marine compasses in compass points only). The compass points used are the four familiar ones: north, east, south and west (N, E, S, W) and the four intermediate points of NE, SE, SW and NW. The compass circle is also divided into 360 degrees. Most compasses are marked every 2°, with actual values shown every 20°. You will need to know only the eight points mentioned.

The working part of the compass is the magnetic *needle*, which will point towards magnetic north. For your purposes you can assume this to be the same as true north. Almost always the *north* end of the needle is dark-coloured, usually red. It is best to check this with another compass before you set out. The following are simple steps that will help you master your compass.

1 To find north, hold the compass flat and steady and away from iron and steel objects. If the compass is held near an iron object such as a pocket knife or belt buckle it may be deflected from north during that time. It can be checked by holding it at several distances from your body just to see if the reading changes. The needle's dark end should point in the same direction regardless of how you rotate the case or how near your body you hold it.

2 To align the case, rotate it until the needle points to the N on the case. If *you also* face the direction the needle is pointing, you will be facing *north*.

3 If you want to find a particular direction other than north—for example, northwest—do not rotate the case but keep the needle of the compass on N and move only your body around the compass until you are looking over the centre of the needle and directly facing the NW mark or 315°.

4 If you want to walk towards the northwest, do not walk *and* watch the compass. Instead, point your body towards the northwest, then carefully pick out a prominent landmark at some distance along this direction. Once spotted, walk towards it. Stop and check your direction

160

from time to time. This is the essence of moving by compass. Simple, isn't it!

Most of the one-day walks require only a map and the guidebook, with the compass not really needed. However, where the way grows indistinct or disappears, the compass comes into its own and the three work together. Where the route skirts a lake or follows a stream or river, the preferred bank to follow will be given as a compass bearing, such as 'the SW shore', 'the N bank'. Sometimes you will be going over a piece of high land, following the bed of one stream up and one down. There must then be a stretch with no watercourse to follow and here the route description will give a compass direction to follow between the two streams. It will also name and describe the land to go over (often as a pass between two easily seen peaks).

One important caveat—ALWAYS BELIEVE YOUR COMPASS. Even experts occasionally become disorientated on cloudy days and swear their compasses have gone wrong. It is easy to get turned around in your sense of direction, especially if you lose sight of known landmarks. Do not panic, just get out your trusty compass and map and get re-orientated.

3   FINDING YOUR WAY IN MIST

This is the most difficult feat in route keeping. It is also a bit unsettling and, very infrequently, can be dangerous. You are most likely to find mist on the ridge tops and mountain summits. If these are cloud-covered at breakfast time but if the weather forecast is just for showers or clearing, it is reasonable to expect the mist to lift later on. However, if a solidly wet day is forecast you should think of a lower-level alternative even if it is by road.

In spite of all your care the mist may suddenly come down and you may be forced to move through it. Here are some recommendations if this should occur:

1   Don't panic—your worst enemy is fear of the mist and not the mist itself.

2   Sit down and wait for a while (but not too long as you will get cold and damp). Find a sheltered spot if possible. Mists can come and go rapidly.

3   While you sit, consult your three best friends: your compass, map and this guidebook. Is going forward or backward the quickest way to lose altitude and thus perhaps get below the mist? Which route direction is better marked (cairns, posts, painted markers or visibly trodden)? Which way has the widest safe swathe of ground to fumble one's way by compass? Is there a stream that can be followed to safety? Check to make sure the stream does not go down over ground that is too steep.

4   If you do decide to move, keep to the path if possible and go slowly. If the way is marked with cairns or posts, move from cairn to cairn or post

to post. Two people help here—one going ahead to find the next post or cairn, the other to stand alone by the last one as a point of reference. Do not go out of voice or whistling range in this search (this is why a whistle is often carried).

5 If you must strike off without benefit of track, cairn or post, use your companion as a landmark by sending him or her ahead along the desired compass heading until he or she is just visible, stopping there until you come up. Repeat the process until clear of the mist. To fine the desired compass heading, if you know your present location roughly and the location you wish to gain, the compass can be used as a protractor, ie a device for measuring angles. The orienteering compass with a movable bezel (ring) and a long, straight side is easiest to use. Lay the map flat and place the compass on it so that the long side points from your present location to the desired point. Rotate the movable bezel until the lines on it point to map north. The desired direction can now be read from the degree mark on the movable bezel that is over the mark on the fixed bezel (the bezels being the rings around the compass needle). With a little more difficulty the cheapest compass can also be used. Place the compass on the map over your present position so that the north mark points in the direction of the new location. Keeping the compass firmly on the map, rotate both until the needle is aligned to map north. Read the bearing under the compass needle and subtract it from 360°. This is your desired compass direction. Since only approximate directions are needed, the differences between magnetic north, map north and true north need not be understood or taken into account. A last word of comfort is that if all the foregoing complicated instructions fly out of your head, our routes are such that you can work to the magnetic cardinal point (N, NE, E, etc) nearest to the direction you want to go and still get safely to civilisation.

4   WALKING TIME

Before you leave for your day's walk it is important to work out how long the expedition is likely to take. You can do this by using your own personal version of what is called the Naismith formula (after the gentleman who first proposed it). The original formula was to divide by 3 the distance in miles that you expected to walk (that is, you were assumed to walk at a base rate of 3mph) and add to that calculated time an additional $\frac{1}{2}$h for every 1000ft of height to be gained. This translates into the metric system by dividing the distance in kilometres by 5 and adding 1.6h for every 1000m of height gained. This is fairly fast walking these days and 2–2½mph plus 1h for every 1000ft of height gained may suit the less experienced walker. This translates into the metric system as 3¼–4kph plus one-third of an hour for every 100m height gained. At the beginning of each of our one-day walks the distance and height gained are noted both in English and metric units. Choose your formula, make your calculations and hope you are not too late for the evening meal.

Note C   Countryside Manners

In brief, countryside manners are simply the Golden Rule applied to the particular circumstances of the countryside. You are sharing the environment with many others—land owners, the Forestry Commission, the National Trust, and other walkers, for example—and you should be sensitive to their rights and needs. Many of us are also coming to believe that the environment itself has rights. A provacative thought. The following list is offered to remind you of the specifics of good countryside manners:

● Respect private property and keep to paths when going through estates and farmland. Where possible, avoid climbing over walls and fences and replace wall stones you might dislodge. CLOSE ALL GATES THAT YOU OPEN. This is easy to forget when your party is of any size, as the gate opener walks on and the last person through may not be aware that it was initially closed. This is best avoided by having the one who opens it stand by to close it.

● Do not leave litter. You might, on occasion, pick up other people's litter.

● Be careful not to disturb sheep in the lambing season (March–May).

● Keep dogs under control, on a lead when requested, especially during the lambing season.

● In forests keep to the paths, avoid smoking and do not light fires. Avoid damaging trees in newly planted forests.

● Safeguard water supplies.

● Protect wildlife and wild plants.

Note D   Safety

The traditional classification of hill walkers is amblers, ramblers, scramblers and danglers. Under this classification, our walks are nearly all in the rambler class, with scrambling extremely rare. In addition, the Walks remain at fairly low altitudes or provide alternatives which do. There is therefore small likelihood of high winds, low temperatures and mists. The Walks are relatively safe from other dangers also—much less dangerous than walking along a busy main road.

Having said all that, it must be added that there are five unlikely but possible dangers that may occur during our Walks and commonsense actions to be taken in their event. These dangers are hypothermia, incapacitating illness or injury, getting lost in the mist, crossing streams and encountering bulls.

163

Hypothermia is a dangerous lowering of body temperature through a combination of low temperature, high wind and poor clothing. The symptoms are incoherent speech, confusion of thought and diminished ability to walk, perhaps leading to occasional falls. The person affected will usually not know that he or she is suffering from it. Prevention is simple—adequate clothing. The remedy is also simple—a hot beverage and some high-energy food (eg sugar or chocolate). If the condition is mild, restoration to normal is immediate. We stress again that hypothermia is most unlikely on our Walks and will not occur with proper clothing. Final insurance is a walking companion and a thermos of hot tea, coffee or cocoa.

We cannot envisage any injury more serious than a turned ankle and, of course, walkers are never ill. However, if you worry about the possibility of becoming incapacitated on the Walk, you should take one or both of two precautions—go in a party of at least 3 (one to stay with the injured person and one to go for help) or inform someone, such as your next night's host, to call for help if you do not appear by an agreed hour. Tell that person where you are starting from and your intended route. Help will come from trained volunteers from the local Mountain Rescue service, which can be contacted through the police (dial 999). In the unlikely event that someone in the party is too ill or injured to move and a member goes for help, it is important to note the map location of the incapacitated member in order to help the rescuers find him or her. The nearest landmark and the distance and direction from it would help. Not only does it aid the rescuers, it can speed the rescue immensely as an exact location may aid in bringing in a helicopter to the site. If you have requested help to be sent in the event of your non-appearance at the expected time, BE SURE TO CALL OFF THE HELP IF IT IS NOT NEEDED (eg if you turn back or simply do not go in the first place). To raise a false alarm and put many people to unnecessary inconvenience is surely a grievous crime among Walkers. For finding your way if lost in the mist or cloud, see Note B Route Finding, p158.

Another possible danger arises when fording streams, especially when they are in spate, ie when greatly swollen by rain. The most general rule is to move upstream until the stream grows sufficiently shallow (as you pass more and more tributaries) to cross with ease. When and where you do finally cross, before you do so, remove your boots, socks and any lower clothing that might get wet (no place for prudery here); put socks and clothing in your rucksack and put the boots back on (wading the rocky bed of a stream in bare feet is just asking for trouble). If in company, link arms, with less muscular members sandwiched between the stronger, and wade across, preferably facing downstream (easier to catch yourself if you stumble). Once across, after a dance of thanksgiving to warm the lower extremities, pour the water out of your boots, resume your clothing, your equanimity and your walk.

A modest danger lies in being charged by irascible bulls; if you are following a right-of-way across green fields and see a bull by itself, it is wisest to give him a wide berth and even stay near a convenient fence or wall as you pass. However, having made you cautious about bulls, we do not want to make you also nervous about cows or bullocks (country-bred people can ignore these remarks). Cows and bullocks are curious by nature, the young ones especially so, and they will often come towards you just to get a better look. A herd of young bullocks, for example, galloping toward you as if they mean never to stop, can be unnerving. Fortunately, their collective curiosity always breaks off well clear of you. What you really want to know is whether the single animal in a herd or a solitary animal is a bull or not. General size is the key: bulls are massive beasts overall and have heavy shoulders and deep chests; these are more certain clues at a distance than the obvious male/female differences.

Note E   Terms Used in Route Descriptions

Footpath signs A sign by the side of the road, pointing in the direction of a public footpath. It denotes a public right-of-way, although many rights-of-way are not so marked. The sign may have a walker symbol or be marked 'Public Footpath' or 'Llwybr Cyhoeddus'. The latter is Welsh for 'public footpath' and we mistook our first such sign as naming and pointing to some place of interest such as a mountain top or waterfall. We searched vainly on the map for the name and the light dawned only as a little further on we encountered other such signs pointing in the opposite direction.

Kissing-gate A 'kissing-gate' or 'scritch-scratch' is a gate for foot traffic only, featuring a small swinging gate operating in a cramped enclosure that foils the foolish sheep, hampers the rucksack-carrying rambler and apparently was once used to ensnare unwary members of the fairer sex, hence 'kissing-gate'. 'Scritch-scratch' comes, we assume, from the noise they make as you pass through. We have shortened the name in our text occasionally to 'k gate', not because we are against kissing but that it might denigrate that pleasant pastime through too much repetition.

Stile A way over a fence or wall that protects both the barrier and the walker and which has the added advantage that it cannot be left open for livestock to wander through. Stiles range from elegant projecting stair-like stones in stone walls to single wood planks, often at inconvenient heights and in dangerous states of decrepitude. Our blessings, neverthe-less, on all stile-makers.

Gate These need no identification as they exist in their thousands everywhere, standard steel or wooden contrivances that open wide enough to let wheeled traffic pass. They must be left as you find them —

open if open, closed if found closed. The ideal gate opens easily to human hands and swings gently on oiled hinges, but that ideal is very rarely found. Locked gates, opening devices rusted fast, hinges missing and replaced by string or wire and gates in various stages of rust or rot will be more common. Many will perforce have to climb over. For the sturdy locked ones this is easy but for those held together by string or habit the climb can be the most dangerous part of your walk. When climbing a gate, it is safer for both you and the gate to climb it at the hinged end as the gate can take the weight better there. Also, don't add to the strain by standing on gates to admire the view.

Roads, lanes, tracks and paths These are the several ways we describe the route and it may not always be clear just what we mean by them. Roads and lanes are metalled or macadam surfaced, the former the normal two-car width, the latter one-car width with passing places (sometimes). Tracks vary from stony, gravel, dirt or grass surfaces but were built for two-wheeled vehicles. Paths are for the feet of humans, horses and other animals. We are not always exact in distinguishing between roads and lanes.

Note F Further Reading

Castles and Historic Places in Wales (Wales Tourist Board 1980)

Drovers' Roads of Wales, Fay Godwin and Shirley Toulson (Wildwood House 1977)

History of the North Wales Slate Industry, Jean Lindsay (David & Charles 1974)

Industrial Archaeology of Wales, David Morgan Rees (David & Charles 1975)

Journey through Wales and Description of Wales, Giraldus Cambrensis (Penguin 1978)

Landscapes of North Wales, Roy Millard and Adrian Robinson (David & Charles 1978)

Life and Tradition in Rural Wales, J. Geraint Jenkins (Dent 1976)

The Mabinogion (Penguin 1976)

National Park Guides: Brecon Beacons, Pembrokeshire Coast, Snowdonia (HMSO)

North Wales Tramways, Keith Turner (David & Charles 1979)

Short History of Wales, A. H. Dodd (Batsford 1977)

Wales: A New Study, (ed) David Thomas (David & Charles 1977)

Welsh Narrow-Gauge Railways, J. D. C. A. Prideaux (David & Charles 1982)

The Welsh Peaks, W. A. Poucher (Constable 1979)

Wild Wales, George Borrow (Collins 1977)

Note G Glossary of Welsh Words in the Text and in Ordnance Survey Maps

aber   mouth of river, confluence of two streams
afon   river
allt   wooded slope, height, hill
bach   small
betws   house of prayer, chapel
blaen (pl **blaenau**)   source of river, head of valley
bryn   hill
bwlch   pass or gap
bychan   little, tiny
capel   chapel
castell   castle
coch   red
coed   wood, trees
cwm   valley
darren   rocky hillside
dinas   hill fortress
du   black
eglwys   church
dyffryn   valley
esgair   ridge
ffridd   mountain pasture, sheep walk
glas   blue, green–grey
glyn   glen or valley
gwyn   white
hafod   summer dwelling
isaf   lowest
llan   church, monastery
llyn   lake
maes   open field, or plain
mawr, fawr   large, big
melyn   yellow
moel   bare hill
mynydd   mountain, moorland
nant   stream, brook
pant   hollow or hill
pen   top, end or head
pentref   village, homestead

pont, bont bridge
pwll pool or pit
rhaeadr waterfall
rhiw Slope, hillside, also a
  slanting path across a hill
rhos moorland
rhyd ford or stream
tal end or front
ty house
tyn smallholding
uchaf highest

We have not attempted to help you to pronounce Welsh words. You will have to turn to a Welsh dictionary such as the *Collins–Spurrell Welsh Dictionary, 1982*, the *Ordnance Survey Place Names on Maps of Scotland and Wales* or one of the small booklets published on the Welsh language. We do urge that you make an honest attempt to learn the more fundamental rules and try to pronounce words, especially place names, as nearly correct as you can. It will be greatly appreciated by your Welsh hosts.

INDEX

Names in italics indicate overnight points on walks. YH indicates a Youth Hostel that serves meals and BBS indicates a Bed Booking Service (see p157) at an overnight point. Page numbers in italics indicate illustrations.

170

171